Advance Praise for
The Stories We Tell Ourselves

When someone shares their trauma in a matter-of-fact way, believe them. That's how it often sounds when you've lived with pain for so long that it just became part of your normal. You stop dramatizing it—not because it didn't hurt, but because it was your life.

That's exactly how I felt reading Tricia Baxley's work—like someone had put words to parts of my own story. Her honesty doesn't beg for pity; it simply offers truth. And in that truth is something deeply comforting: the reminder that we're not alone, and that healing—real, lasting healing—is still possible, no matter how long it's been.

This book isn't just insightful. It's a companion. Tricia offers guidance with such care and clarity that it feels like she's walking right beside you. What a gift for anyone who's ever wondered if it was too late to come home to themselves.

—Rose Baker, Columbus, OH

The Stories We Tell Ourselves is a sacred companion for anyone who has walked through heartbreak and wondered if light could still live within them. Tricia's vulnerability is breathtaking—she doesn't just share her story, she opens her soul. Despite the trials, what radiates most is her unwavering positivity, a quiet astonishment that beauty can still grow from pain. Her resilience isn't loud—it's holy. Through every page, she offers not just words but a lived pathway to healing. I closed this book, not only moved, but it reminded me that wholeness is possible.

—Mary Greene, Gahanna, OH

This book is one of the most honest and compassionate guides I've ever encountered. It doesn't pretend to fix you—it walks beside you as you find your way back to yourself. The author's vulnerability is a gift, and her wisdom is hard-earned. Every page felt like a conversation with someone who has truly lived what they teach. If you're ready to heal gently and deeply, this book is a sacred place to begin.

—Samantha Rizzo, Bensalem, PA

In *The Stories We Tell Ourselves*, Tricia has written about her past painful experiences and life to serve as an example of dysfunction. She is boldly and courageously honest with both the reader and herself, serving as a guide to help heal others. She also provides a workbook, *Rewriting the Stories that Shape Our Lives*, with exercises to expertly guide the reader through the process to begin healing themselves.

If you come from or are in a dysfunctional (toxic) family/environment or are wanting to process through childhood and or adult experiences, I highly recommend this book and workbook!

Personally, Tricia is one of the most loving, giving, truthful, and authentic individuals I know, and I am blessed to have her in my life experience. The work and information she has given in this book and workbook, I believe, are truly Divinely inspired.

—Nancy Kirchhofer, Westerville, OH

The Stories We Tell Ourselves and the accompanying workbook, *Rewriting the Stories that Shape Our Lives*, are unquestionably two of the most painful yet ultimately beautiful books I've ever read, or ever hope to read.

Tricia's core message seems to be that no matter the depths of our tragedy or heartbreak, there's always a way out, and Tricia, through the example of her very own life, is here to help us to do exactly that. I also think that her books are about the invincible strength of the human spirit, which lives not only in Tricia's heart but also in all of us as we follow her lead and transcend our pain and fears by living a courageous life of soulful authenticity, honesty, and love.

It's so cliché to say that someone has "talked the talk," "walked the walk," or "swam the swamp," but to say that Tricia's childhood was much like traversing a swamp of perpetually traumatizing heartache could actually be considered a pitiful understatement. Within the firestorm of Tricia's torment, she displays a drive to search within herself and to help us to do the same in order to find our soul's higher purpose, regardless of the travesties which we may have endured.

The devastating and heartbreaking stories that Tricia recounts in gut-wrenching detail throughout the forlorn pages of her memoir takes us (her readers) by the hand, walks us through the darkness, and then shows us by example how a commitment from the depths of her heart to live a life of love, authenticity, and honesty has brought a lasting solace to even the most dire of her traumatic wounds.

For anyone (like me) who has endured extreme pain in their life, I wholeheartedly recommend both Tricia's memoir and her workbook, as I believe they provide us not only an honest glimpse of hope but also a transcendent path of light through even the darkest of our nights.

—Doug Fitzsimmons, Centerville, OH
Doctor of Physical Therapy

Identifying and reinterpreting the unquestioned beliefs about ourselves, however they may have been formed, is key to our freedom to be whole and happy.

With courage and honesty, Tricia shares her painful imprisonment within her own defenses and beliefs, and how she ultimately released her Self to fully Be.

In the accompanying workbook, *Rewriting the Stories that Shape Our Lives,* developed through her experiences, she offers a helpful guide to liberation from our own harmful and limiting stories.

—Katherine Jones, Fairborn, OH

Tricia Baxley's book and companion workbook are gifts for anyone wanting to better understand and grow from their not-so-pleasant life circumstances.

You'll know that Tricia had a childhood with seemingly insurmountable obstacles. The phrase "what doesn't kill you makes you stronger" certainly applies. Fortunately, the trials and tribulations of Tricia's life have enabled her to write a book and a companion workbook that will enable anyone to better understand the causes and effects more fully in their own life and be guided through a deep, life-enhancing healing process.

The Stories We Tell Ourselves reads like a suspense novel, and *Rewriting the Stories that Shape Our Lives* gives everyone an actionable guide to get the most growth from their own challenges, enabling many to transition from surviving to thriving.

—Rich Cordale, Columbus, OH

In this memoir of awakening from a disturbing past, Tricia Baxley has told her story through remembered moments and events beginning at age 6 when her mother attempted suicide. The author uses intuition, self-observation, spiritual guidance, books, and therapy to interpret herself.

Influenced by Dr. David Hawkins, *A Course in Miracles*, and Carl Jung, among others, she has found her way to peace. Her journey is deeply inspiring, and her workbook provides a clear and compassionate framework that others can follow to begin their own healing, just as Tricia has.

—Gail A. Lichtenfels, Master of Humanities, Yellow Springs, OH

The Stories We Tell Ourselves and the guided workbook, *Rewriting the Stories that Shape Our Lives*, are profound! That is the first word that came into my soul upon completion of reading it. Tricia's book and guide are rich in meaning and insight, going beyond the surface level and touching the truths within one's soul. Together, the book and the workbook form a sacred journey.

In my work in the leadership side of the healthcare world over the years, I have learned and seen that there is even a greater epidemic in our world than the coronavirus pandemic we faced: mental illness, depression, and addiction. I believe God aligns the stars in the sky and connects the dots of our lives. He connected my life to Tricia Baxley, a GOD APPOINTMENT!

Along with the coronavirus came the mandate to wear masks. Some people loved wearing the masks, while others protested strongly against them. As I reflect back, I wonder if those who wore the masks without protest felt a sense of comfort in wearing them because, in life, invisible masks are often worn for protection, yet those masks can keep us prisoners.

Tricia literally shares with us the process of removing her masks, "The soul journey to uncovering the hidden scripts that define us." She encourages us with her story and the guided workbook to remove the invisible masks we wear. If we become comfortable with being uncomfortable, we will be set free, finding a freedom we have never known and a comfort for our souls that will never end. Take a sacred journey, a walk by faith, not by sight, and the Spirit will indeed set you free! Indeed, you will be set free.

—Marilyn R. Beverley
President of the Board of Directors
Munising Memorial Hospital

The Stories We Tell Ourselves

THE SOUL JOURNEY TO UNCOVERING THE HIDDEN SCRIPTS THAT DEFINE US

The Stories We Tell Ourselves

THE SOUL JOURNEY TO UNCOVERING THE HIDDEN SCRIPTS THAT DEFINE US

Tricia Baxley

ethos collective

The Stories We Tell Ourselves © 2025 by Tricia Baxley.
All rights reserved.

Printed in the United States of America

Published by Igniting Souls
PO Box 43, Powell, OH 43065
IgnitingSouls.com

This book contains material protected under international and federal copyright laws and treaties. Any unauthorized reprint or use of this material is prohibited. No part of this book may be reproduced or transmitted in any form or by any means, electronic or mechanical, including photocopying, recording, or by any information storage and retrieval system, without express written permission from the author.

LCCN: 2025905327
Paperback ISBN: 978-1-63680-489-7
Hardcover ISBN: 978-1-63680-490-3
e-book ISBN: 978-1-63680-491-0

Available in paperback, hardcover, e-book, and audiobook.

Any Internet addresses (websites, blogs, etc.) and telephone numbers printed in this book are offered as a resource. They are not intended in any way to be or imply an endorsement by Igniting Souls, nor does Igniting Souls vouch for the content of these sites and numbers for the life of this book.

Some names and identifying details may have been changed to protect the privacy of individuals.

To my two beautiful boys, Kevin and Ryan,
the greatest honor of my life has been to be your Mom.
Your love, your spirit, and your hearts have filled my world with meaning.
You are my inspiration and my joy, and I am forever grateful for you both.

This book is for you,
and for the many relationships that have nourished us,
lifted us through challenges, and surrounded us with love.
These connections have been our source of strength,
and they continue to remind us of what truly matters.

With all my Love,
Mom

Table of Contents

Foreword by Reverend Clarence Campbell............................xv
Preface xix
Introduction xxi

Panel One
The Stories I Inherited

Chapter 1 3
Chapter 2 8
Chapter 3 14
Chapter 4 19
Chapter 5 25
Chapter 6 31
Chapter 7 36
Chapter 8 40
Chapter 9 49

Panel Two
The Stories I Lived

Chapter 1 57
Chapter 2 63
Chapter 3 71
Chapter 4 80

Chapter 5 86
Chapter 6 95
Chapter 7 102
Chapter 8 109
Chapter 9 117
Chapter 10 135
Chapter 11 140
Chapter 12 148
Chapter 13 156
Chapter 14 160

Panel Three
Rewriting the Story

Chapter 1 165
Chapter 2 177
Chapter 3 184
Chapter 4 192
Chapter 5 198
Chapter 6 206
Chapter 7 211
Chapter 8 217
Chapter 9 222
Chapter 10 228
Chapter 11 234

Acknowledgments 241
About the Author 245

Foreword by Reverend Clarence Campbell

AS WE TRAVEL on our journey—more like an odyssey into the unknown—we encounter certain people who stop us in our tracks. Tricia Baxley is one of those people. It's like a holy encounter described in *A Course in Miracles*—there's a familiarity that feels immediate and unmistakable, as if Soul recognizes Soul.

I met Tricia through the *A Course in Miracles* class I facilitate every Sunday morning. She joined us just before the COVID-19 pandemic began. Over the years, a friendship blossomed between us, rooted in deep spiritual inquiry and truth-seeking conversations. We often explored topics that spiritual seekers must confront in order to ascend the ladder of awareness. Our discussions were real—sometimes raw—and always anchored in the courage to be honest, not only with others but most importantly with ourselves.

This book that Tricia has written is a deeply personal story of discovering her "true" Self. As she looked back on her life, she revisited the places where she overcame and the places where she didn't. She examined the trials, traumas, and moments of grace that have shaped her. And in that reflection, she found meaning—not just in what she survived, but in how she transformed.

Tricia manages to rise above deeply painful moments in her life—experiences that could have broken her—and she uses them instead to forge her destiny. Her story reminds me of a gospel song titled "How I Got Over." A key lyric says: *My soul looks back and wonders how I got over.* That's the spirit of this book—a soul reflecting, not with bitterness, but with awe.

With searing honesty, Tricia walks us through the inner architecture of her resilience: from a challenging relationship with her parents, to surviving a marriage with an alcoholic, to the profound loss of her husband. Her life has not been easy, but she held it together through heartbreak, faith, and a fierce determination to rise.

She lays it all out for us—the hurt, the pain, the tears—for all to see. This is a soul-baring, unapologetically raw account of a life lived and re-examined. Why tell this story? Because in telling the truth, she offers others a chance to heal. Her courage becomes a mirror for our own.

In this book, Tricia moves from self to Self—from the fragmented to the whole. She reminds me of the voice in Adrienne Rich's poem "Diving into the Wreck." Listen to these words:

> *I came to explore the wreck.*
> *The words are purposes.*
> *The words are maps.*
> *I came to see the damage that was done,*
> *And the treasures that prevail.*

This book is a treasure—one offered by a survivor who left behind a ladder for the rest of us. That ladder is her workbook, Rewriting The Stories We Tell Ourselves, a tool for anyone ready to climb out of their own wreckage and into their truth.

In closing, let us remember the words of Socrates: *"The unexamined life is not worth living."*

Tricia's work is not just a book. It's an invitation.

To look again.
To dive deeper.
To tell the truth.
And to rise.

—Reverend Clarence Campbell
Associate Pastor, 1st Christian Spiritualist Church

Preface

TO SAY I'VE lived a crazy life would be an extreme understatement. To say it's been crazier than most, it's hard to say. I have always believed that by the end of each of our lives, we all have had our own fair share of challenges to overcome. Personally, I have been through so many emotional challenges, beginning in early childhood until nine years ago. It's hard to believe that I somehow came out relatively whole.

This book is being written because, through my own personal journey and healing, I realize there was actually a "master plan." While life seemed random, there was a Divine Purpose behind everything that has happened to me and the choices I have made throughout my life because of these events.

It is my premise that we experience our own specific difficulties in childhood, and that these challenges pave the way for our spiritual growth. Each of us will bring our own set of Soul challenges to this lifetime, so comparing lives will never make sense. Where we are on our own Soul journey will never be the same as anyone else's.

I have always been a deep-thinking person, even in my darkest hours, believing that I would survive. Gratitude has always been a cornerstone of my life, and it is one of my greatest God-given gifts. Even as a small child, I pondered the deeper questions, such as "Why are we here?" and "What is the purpose of life?" I often forced myself to stop out of frustration when the answers were not forthcoming. I grew up with a unique way of viewing my life here on earth. This journey, while different from everyone else's, as each of our paths is unique, has provided incredible growth. This has given me a framework to help others on similar paths.

Through the course of thousands of hours with spiritual advisors and psychics Rosalie Strawcutter (clairvoyant medium, inventor), Laura Scott (channeler, healer, mystic), Julie North (medium and medical intuitive), Bee Herz (psychic medium) and Rebecca Manns (psychic medium), I believe that our main purpose for being here is to grow our Souls, to become whole, and to connect to the Divine that is the core in all of us. When I now look back on my life and the subsequent choices I have made, I can see how perfectly it unfolded. I realize that had I learned these lessons sooner, I could have become my best self without the decades of heartache. My story, both a memoir and a self-help process, is a story of hope and healing. I strongly feel that my experience needs to be shared so others can live a more joyful and love-filled life much sooner.

Introduction

THROUGH MY EXPERIENCES, I have developed my belief system and have had the blessings of being in contact with deceased loved ones, spirit guides, guardian angels, and past life themes that have carried into this lifetime. While I have a very developed belief system, which I will explain, the value of this book is not reliant on you adopting all or any of the same beliefs.

I have always had a spiritual counselor and believe the "other side" can assist us on our journey. This doesn't mean that what we see will happen, because free will always prevails, but instead, it reveals the energetic possibility, both good and bad. As early as my twenties, I can recall going to a palm reader on the Atlantic City Boardwalk and being told I would have two boys, an idea I laughed at since I was ambivalent about having children at that point.

Decades later, I was visiting my late friend Louise Cueva in Santa Monica, a "psychic to the stars," and while reading my cards, she saw me having two boys as well. She said I would inherit from Mother, which was ludicrous since she was financially dependent on me, and that I would inherit money from someone at work. All suggestions seemed preposterous. I was in my early 40s with one child, yet six months later, I conceived my second son. My mother left money, and thirteen years later, I received an inheritance from someone at work.

During the past nine years, I have been fortunate to really delve into my spiritual life and find answers to the questions that have been plaguing me since childhood. My first discovery is that we are here to grow our Souls, to become the best authentic version of ourselves through deep, unconditional self-love with the help of God's Unconditional Love, a feat I learned is much harder than the words appear.

The "gift of life" we all talk about is truly a gift; it allows us here on earth to have contrast—Love/hate, joy/sorrow, happiness/sadness. In the afterlife, contrast doesn't exist. It is only Love and Light, so while growth can happen, it can happen much quicker and more profoundly here.

During early adulthood, I consistently sought a connection to the spiritual side of myself and life; however, the path I chose for financial stability versus spiritual passion and fulfillment kept pulling me further away from my true self, my Higher Power, and inner guidance. I have always believed in the afterlife and that life was more than we realized here on Earth, though I never took the time to reflect on what this actually meant to me.

In 2016, life threw me a curveball I never imagined could happen, and it was at this point that I got really serious about my spiritual journey. It has blessed me with finding the right people at the right time to help me on my path, a blessing we all share if we will listen to our internal voice or Higher Self.

My second understanding is that everything on this earth and in the universe is connected and interconnected on an energetic Soul level. If I hurt you, I am also hurting myself as well as everyone else on this planet, and even further. Every action, thought, and emotion from the beginning of life—past, present, and future—is recorded in the Akashic Records/Book of Knowledge/Universal Consciousness.

The Akashic Record is the source of everything that has ever happened to each of us on a Soul level. It is from these records that I have learned the details of my most recent incarnations on earth, and this has enlightened me to how we, as humans, live our lives largely unconsciously.

Some say that our entire base of knowledge is like grains of sand on the beach, and our consciousness is only a grain or two of sand. This means we are making major life choices—careers, life partners, where to live, etc.—mostly blind and often based on beliefs we have learned in previous lifetimes and from others along the way while on Earth, beginning in childhood.

Sadly, these beliefs are not always true, and they are often influenced by our families, peers, teachers, coaches, religious upbringing, and society's programming and conditioning. We need to see these false beliefs for what they are to allow ourselves to become whole, a wholeness that is already within us.

In this book, I will show you my life as it unfolded, the unconscious programming that dictated every decision, and the steps I took to change my story about myself. I've tested the process. It works, and it will set you on the path to becoming more conscious yourself, making your journey much more joyful, calm, and meaningful, and helping you discover your own life's purpose.

I have written this book in what I call three panels: childhood, which sets the groundwork for our spiritual growth; young adult; and then middle age and beyond. When we cross over, many of us have a conviction that we will have a life review. We will look into a pool of water and see our life from birth until death, where we failed and where we succeeded. My loved ones who have passed have explained to me that our life review is really in panels, which is what I have called my life stages in this book.

These life stages are the same for all of us, and it's why we all will eventually go through a "midlife crisis" in one form or another, which is really just a "push" from our Soul and

Universe to get us to wake up spiritually. It was also explained to me that as we do our life review, we will also experience, judgment-free, how we affected others, good and bad, and how those actions affect us emotionally.

We will also experience the effects of others' behavior on us as well as their emotional reactions, which serve to provide insight, healing, and growth from our experiences here. With insight into everyone else's perspective, as they have lived our life alongside us, it allows us to experience compassion and understanding, and ultimately, forgiveness.

Forgiveness is the foundation of Unconditional Love, and by changing the lens through which we see the world and others, we can transcend childhood programming and experience the connectedness of being one with the world and everyone in it.

My third lesson from my spiritual journey is that the people we meet in our lives are purposeful and not by accident, though it might seem like every encounter is random. Every single person from my childhood onward has had a hand in my spiritual growth. Ironically, the people who have caused the greatest pain have afforded me the most profound growth. People either mirror our Soul and wisdom or mirror our woundedness.

It is my belief that before reincarnating, which is a choice each Soul makes, we decide what lessons we need to work on. The lessons will dictate when we are born, which parents we pick to facilitate these lessons, what body type, the personality we will have, and the people in our lives who will support us, hurt us, and challenge us to help us grow.

I realize that for many of you, the idea that we pick our parents might seem outrageous; however, for me, I have confirmed this in hours of afterlife readings. It makes sense to me because otherwise, how does one reconcile an all-loving God allowing babies to be born into environments where there will never be enough food, and ultimately, they will starve to death?

It is my understanding that these brave Souls asked for the challenge of destitution and starvation and, by doing so, on a Soul level, learned the emotions behind the lack of basic human needs. We all are striving for wholeness, and even a starving baby in a developing country has the same opportunity for connecting to his or her Divine, though arguably under dire conditions.

They are also doing a tremendous service to humanity by raising our collective consciousness to understand that we are all connected, and therefore, we have to care about a starving baby in another part of the world that we will never know. This teaches others compassion, service, and empathy—what a selfless act on a Soul level to agree to suffer to allow others to grow!

Hard to imagine, but based on the laws of quantum physics, we energetically connect to everyone and everything in the Universe. A starving child in a third-world country does indeed affect each of us energetically, even if we are unaware of it. It is very easy to assume that who we are on Earth is who we are and that our earthly body defines us. I often refer to a quote by Pierre Teilhard de Chardin: "We are not human beings having a spiritual experience; we are spiritual beings having a human experience." This is the basis for my book.

PANEL ONE

The Stories I Inherited

*Imprints of fear, survival, and separation—
written before I had a voice.*

Chapter 1

It's not the actual trauma and events from childhood that cause the most damage. It's the unconscious beliefs about ourselves, often formed in childhood from the trauma, that have the greatest negative impact.

❇

EACH OF US enters childhood innocent and unblemished. Even under the best of circumstances, life can leave us bruised and often worse by the time we are ready to leave the nest. Some of us knew our families were ill-equipped to raise children; others lived with the illusion that their family was perfect. I often ponder which is worse, the knowing or the illusion?

In my case, it was unmistakable from the age of six and a half that my parents were not qualified on their best day. Conversely, someone who has lived with the illusion that their family was perfect when perfection doesn't exist will often repeat the same family patterns until they wake up spiritually. It's easy to see how dysfunctional cycles continue through many generations.

For the first ten years of my life, we lived in a small housing development in Mystic, CT, and in those days, most kids walked to and from school. One day, my brothers and I walked home like three little ducks in a row, as we always did—my older brother, David, eleven months older than me, I at six and a half, and my younger brother, Kenny, at five; Bruce was still an infant. I believe that each of us has significant events that shape our unconscious, and, sadly, mine happened at a very young age.

That day was nothing extraordinary until we walked into the house, searched for Mom, and found her sitting on her favorite chair, attempting suicide by slicing her wrists as if all mothers greet their kids in this manner. To this day, I can still see the image, the look of disinterest on Mother's face, and, more notably, the towel on the chair. Even at that young age, it didn't escape me that Mother took the time to protect her chair but was oblivious to the need to protect her children. As an adult, I was told my brother David ran to the neighbors while I screamed. Eventually, neighbors ushered me out of the house, and I stayed with a neighbor for the rest of the night.

As you can probably imagine, my life as an innocent child came to a screeching halt; even then I knew a few things about how my life was going to be moving forward: 1) Mother was not emotionally strong; 2) Mother could never protect me; 3) No one has my back; 4) The beginning of the knowledge that I needed to be strong for everyone so this didn't happen again. These are the lessons I learned that I was conscious of. The lessons that really dictated my life and caused the most damage were the limiting beliefs and wounds I wasn't aware of.

Back in those days, therapy was never a consideration, so Mother went away for a few days, and from an outsider's perspective, we went back to the way it was before, never to be mentioned again. The problem was, it never went back to the way it was before; you can't destroy and then recover a child's innocence. Each of us reacted in our own way, according to our personalities. David became more introverted, while Kenny, too young to understand the implications, told everyone what had happened. I, on the other hand, became the perfect daughter. This was the beginning of the codependency that was my traveling companion until nine years ago.

This was the immediate fallout of what we witnessed, but these types of trauma seem to have a rippling effect. I can remember a few months later getting a ride home from school. By now, everyone knew our family secret. Thankfully, I was still too young to recognize this.

My neighbor asked if what Kenny had told her about Mother "cutting her wrist" was true. For a split second, surprise took me, and then I knew I had to cover it up, so I lied and said he was mistaken, and it was an accident.

On this day, the rippling effect taught me: 1) we must keep our family secrets safe, lying if necessary, and 2) we must bury our shame. As a result, lying about my family became a common occurrence—my shame, a favorite sidekick to my codependency.

Not every childhood is as dramatic as this, and believe me, this is just the beginning for me. However, even smaller things make us believe negative things about ourselves. Mother had two kids by the time she was seventeen, three by nineteen, and as an unwed mother, which I didn't know about until many years later, she was very overwhelmed and already spiraling out of control. Mother truly had no clue about raising toddlers. How could she when she was still a child herself?

Two stories stand out. One, Mother wanted me to take a nap when I was about two years old. I was very high energy and strong-willed, maybe the worst fit for my low-energy mother on her best day, and I can remember her chasing me around a big, long station wagon and knowing inside my head that she could never catch me. She eventually gave up.

The message this taught me was that I was much stronger physically, and that Mother had given up; I was already making a subconscious list of what I wanted to be like. Years later, I discovered I had an aptitude for running, and my desire for not being like Mother, for not giving up, stemmed all the way back to this day. As you'll learn later, while I excelled at running, which was an obvious positive, there was a downside to this as well.

Another early memory that helped shape my belief system happened when I was three. I grew up in the sixties, and we, like many families, had a coffee table with razor-sharp edges. Baby proofing was not a "thing" in those days, and keeping the kids safe at all, for Mother, was not a "thing" either.

Even then, Mother spent a lot of time smoking cigarettes and drinking coffee—the alcohol didn't come until later—leaving David and me to our own devices. One of our favorite pastimes was chasing each other around the coffee table; today, we would never let our young kids near this table.

At one point, David fell, cut the corner of his eye, and had to get stitches. Mother's way of looking at things, to avoid a similar accident, was to simply not look at them. Fast forward a few weeks, and this time I hit the center of my forehead and needed stitches. What I vividly recall is that Mother was so angry over the inconvenience, and that I never cried.

I remember sitting at the kitchen table with the washcloth on my forehead, trying to choke down my oatmeal so we could then go to the hospital and have the cut stitched. There was no sympathy forthcoming from Mother, no concern, and no sense that avoiding this was within her control. I remember feeling so bad for getting hurt and ruining Mother's day.

I internalized this flawed feeling my entire life. On the outside, I was the picture of success and high self-esteem, but buried deep in the crevices of my being, I felt like a bad little girl. Even writing this after healing makes me so sad, mostly because of the realization that my beliefs about myself began long before I could challenge them.

I believe we all have limiting beliefs that our unconscious keeps and ultimately dictates every decision we make until we confront, grieve, and then heal ourselves. To put it mildly, the scar on my forehead that I have carried my entire life is nothing compared to the scar I've carried in my psyche.

Chapter 2

What do you do when you're a child and the person you need to go to to feel better is the very person who is hurting you?

❈

MY PARENTS REALLY did not know how to parent, though, as an adult, I realize they did the best they could. Despite this, I am still shocked at how miserably they fell short. We used to go camping as kids, which was never fun because the dysfunction never stayed behind. It always joined us.

In a campground, when you knew no one, we really had no way to escape. One summer, we traveled to the border of Canada. I was around 7, and it was a French holiday while we were there. My parents had a dilemma: go to the celebration or take care of the kids. As you probably guessed, they went to the party, sneaking out while we were asleep in the camper.

I woke up to pitch black. With no parents and at seven years old, I had to find the communal bathroom on my own in an unfamiliar campground. There was a long line of adult partygoers waiting, so I got in line with them. Not one person spoke English, and it petrified me as they tried communicating with me and touching my hair, which was long and curly. They literally scared me to death.

I finally made it to the front of the line, went to the bathroom, and then bolted back to the camper. It was a miracle I found my way, and this is where my independence began. To this day, I have never told my parents about what happened. I didn't want them to be angry that I left on my own. It never occurred to me that I should have been angry.

Camping stories abound in our family. In fairness, back then, my parents didn't have access to the internet, so they never fact-checked their decisions against logic to make sure traveling to a specific place made sense.

By the time I was six, we were a family of six, and traveling anywhere was an ordeal. My parents had no patience, smoked like fiends, and made every outing stressful. Driving any distance, much less six or more hours to a vacation spot that was anything but a vacation, really wasn't something any of us kids looked forward to.

On one hand, I have to hand it to Mother. She always had the idealism that this vacation was going to be different this time, that somehow all the daily dysfunction would vanish since we were in the forest of Maine. Obviously, it never played out this way.

What is so interesting is that long before I understood karma and the Law of Attraction, that we attract in what we put out, or, said another way, we attract who and what we are energetically, I knew intuitively that my parents created their own "bad luck."

One year, we traveled to Bar Harbor, Maine, which we had done for years, only to find that the lake was bone dry. The entire purpose of the camping trip was to have a campsite on the lake, the kids can go play on their own, and the parents can drink themselves silly. Well, this was an enormous setback.

What to do with the kids to keep them occupied?

It never crossed their minds to go home, so instead, they found brackish ponds around the campsite and told us to go play in them instead. Seemed like a great idea, except each day we would come back at night—we got used to literally going out in the morning and not coming back until dinner, both at home or when away—covered with leeches!

Our parents treated this as normal, so we did too. Clearly, not normal! My independence continued to grow on these adventures, and my ability to handle bugs, snakes, frogs, and lizards grew exponentially compared with most kids my age.

Another memorable vacation was again in Maine, when Mother decided she needed to go to the store, and by now, I was being dragged along constantly. I really hated going with her because she was so rude, and her unhappiness kept people far away, but I was too afraid of her at this point to assert myself.

On this day, she took me to help her find her way, which was ridiculous since I sat in the back seat on most excursions around the camp, focusing on not getting car sick so I didn't get yelled at; I was not the person to be navigating! Eventually, Mother got lost and asked me if we should go right or left, and since it was a fifty-fifty answer. I picked right, which ultimately proved wrong.

We ended up on a beach, and to this day, I cannot fathom what would possess Mother to drive on a beach with a massive station wagon, but she did, and within minutes, we were in sand up to the windows. I was then screamed at to go get help because, in Mother's words, "This was all your fault," and yet again, the future runner in me was called in alongside the shame-filled codependent.

I distinctly remember berating myself for choosing the wrong way. What was worse was that it took approximately ten adults to dig us out, while my mother blamed it all on me.

Being blamed was nothing new, but the embarrassment and shame of having strangers help us and exposing them to our messed-up family was horrible. By now, my primary goal with my parents was that they didn't cause a scene. Neutrality was always a win in my book.

✸ ✸ ✸

When one figures out at a young age that she is more emotionally mature than their parents, all kinds of beliefs ensue, many of which are detrimental in the long run.

Sound judgment was something my parents always lacked. If there were two decisions, inevitably they seemed to pick the worse one. Besides lacking emotional skills, both parents lacked rational thought, and even at a very young age, their poor decision-making skills amazed me.

By the time I was in elementary school, because of so much emotional hurt and pain, I learned to shut down my feelings in favor of rational thought. This was both a blessing and a curse when I was finally old enough to leave the nest; however, while I was still under my parents' control, it was a gift that literally kept me sane.

An example of my parents' lack of rational thought is that they decided a wonderful idea would be to get a dog. Now, mind you, a dog in a family with kids is a wonderful idea. I currently have a great dog named Lilly, but when you're not even taking care of your kids, and financial resources are scarce, a dog just doesn't make sense.

To make matters worse, my parents took in an abused Saint Bernard, and though admirable on one level, he was extremely skittish, a huge shedder, and drooled unmercifully. I always thought it ironic how proud my parents were that they saved an abused dog while they continued to neglect their own children. Denial is an amazing defense mechanism. For a few days, the family dilemma was what to name the "new family member," and they finally called our new dog Jumbo, which was more than fitting.

Jumbo became a member of our household a week before our annual camping trip to Maine, and it wasn't until Jumbo was home that they realized the predicament this posed. After weighing all the options, which probably never happened, they got the genius idea of taking the dog with us and driving six hours with him in the camper we were towing since there was no room in the car.

By now, I was already not a fan of Jumbo. He smelled like a dog and got more positive attention than the kids; he got fed more consistently, and the drool was just plain disgusting. As you might have guessed, no one asked my opinion. So we traveled for six hours. As usual, I focused on not getting car sick. My brothers fought, my parents screamed at us, and every once in a while, you would hear Jumbo take a fall on a sharp corner and yelp.

When we finally arrived, we all piled out of the car, and my parents were shocked—yes, shocked—that Jumbo had both urinated and defecated several times, destroying the camper. Still, we stayed the week while my parents drank like fiends, blaming each other for the camper damage, and we probably ruined everyone else's trip too, since yelling at a campground became everyone's business.

By now, I had learned to block it all out, and in the morning, when I saw our neighbors at the showers, I acted like nothing had transpired the night before. I had become so good at disassociating and burying my shame that I literally did not feel a thing. The problem is, I was feeling so much below the surface that I didn't realize it.

On the way home from this trip, my parents debated about putting a kid in the camper—yes, this was an actual discussion—and they thankfully shoved the dog in the already filled-to-the-brim station wagon. This is one of the few times I actually recall complaining; the slime from Jumbo's mouth was just too much for me to handle, so the solution was for me to sit in the packed front seat, literally pressed against the dashboard as Jumbo drooled over the seat where I was supposed to be sitting.

Not once did my parents acknowledge that the timing of adopting Jumbo was a poor decision, and consequently, my childhood was littered with equally poor parental decisions because my parents refused to learn from their mistakes.

Chapter 3

*Childhood left me with a gaping, painful hole
in my heart that good, loving parents and a
normal, safe childhood should have filled.*

❉

AFTER MOTHER'S SUICIDE attempt, we got back to living our lives as if it had never happened. Looking back, I was painfully aware I was on my own and behaved accordingly. The covert message I received was that I needed to do everything possible so that Mother wouldn't try to kill herself again. I became the "good girl." I would go to school, and once it was over, relieve Mother of taking care of my youngest brother, Bruce.

Others often praised me for being such a helper, which fed my need to help others above myself. It was this praise that fostered my belief that I was indeed "good" and not "bad," and the only way to stay "safe" was to be perfect and to do whatever was needed.

While I picked up slack for Mother (I was now conditioned to believe Mother had it so hard, and I felt so sorry for such an unfortunate life given to her), she took the free time to drink to self-medicate her problems away.

Home life became predictably unpredictable and, mostly, fairly under control, though dysfunctional. Neighbors were always willing to have me over for dinner. Of course, I was the perfect guest, always willing to help, and by now, I was becoming more comfortable talking to adults than kids my age.

Turns out that while my actions became more parental, my ability to relate to kids my age became harder. At every step of the way, adults praised me for my maturity, and this made me feel both proud and powerful. This was the beginning of my seeking outside accolades to build my shaky self-esteem. Fortunately, years later, I got knocked off this pedestal, or I might have become a narcissist instead of a codependent.

From the volumes of books I have read, therapy, and conversations with those on the other side, I have learned that it is rare for one to come out of my family dynamic still having their Self-Love intact. I feel blessed that I became codependent, which is really the flip side of becoming a narcissist.

Both have enormous holes inside of them, both suffer deep self-esteem issues, both are emotionally unavailable, both have trust issues, and both look outside themselves for validation. The biggest difference between the two is that the narcissist is a taker, and the codependent is a giver.

Many years ago, I was seeing a therapist who also taught other therapists, and he asked if I would be a patient during a teaching session with the therapists. I jumped at the chance because I was determined to get better, and I appreciated any help. What struck me as interesting was that even the seasoned therapists had a hard time seeing the damage codependency had done to me and others, since I was professionally successful, had wonderful kids, and had a solid support system in place.

It occurred to me, which I verbalized, that many overlook codependency as different than other mental health issues because most people, including many healthcare professionals, perceive a giver as positive and, therefore, socially acceptable. What they were missing was that while the narcissist damages others, the damage to oneself was equally bad for the codependent and enabling others just continued the dysfunctional cycle.

Both are living unauthentically and from their wounded self. It's how my challenges stayed under the radar most of my life. I was helping the rest of the world while I was destroying myself. The worst part is that I never knew until nine years ago how lost I actually was.

✽ ✽ ✽

Changing your home without changing your beliefs, thoughts, and feelings changes nothing. The problems, false beliefs, and trauma get packed right along with everything else.

As time went on, my parents got the brilliant idea that we should move. On one hand, I felt this was a great idea since now I was around nine years old and was becoming painfully aware that everyone knew about Mother's suicide attempt. Both parents started drinking more heavily and became even more neglectful of us, which furthered my embarrassment and shame.

I started having nightmares, which made perfect sense considering everything, and one very late night, I ended up in the middle of the street. A neighbor had gotten up in the middle of the night, saw me in the street, and brought me home. Mother's response was anger that I woke her up and that I embarrassed her; she never asked about the dream, which was actually a nightmare and mirrored my life perfectly.

Slowly but surely, I was being taught that fear, sadness, anger, disappointment, frustration, and annoyance, to name a few, were not acceptable emotions. Conversely, I found my false self reinforced at every step, and I willingly complied for the sake of survival, being programmed over and over that my role was to be a supportive caretaker, always happy, never asking for anything.

For most of my childhood, I had a recurring dream almost nightly. It was me in a free fall with no one to catch me: a perfect symbol of how I felt inside, though consciously denied.

Weekends were now spent piling into the station wagon to visit potential new homes, parents smoking non-stop, no conversation, and me trying not to vomit. This went on for several months, and to say my brothers and I hated it was an understatement.

My parents criticized anything that was outside the perfection they were looking for or that demanded their involvement. This is where each of our roles solidified. David became the scapegoat since he refused to play the game. I became the golden child and peacemaker because I played the game. As the middle child, Kenny was neglected and completely overlooked by Mother and Father. Bruce, though the baby, was still neglected.

I need to add here that regardless of our role, none of us got our emotional needs met, and often, not even our physical needs. The roles were both inherited and our individual reaction to a stressful environment, but none served any of us well in the long run.

Even though I got more accolades because I was the peacemaker and helper, it was because of my sensitivity that this role made sense. The problem is, I had to bury my deep sensitivity to survive, and this caused so much damage on a Soul level and again affected every career choice and relationship throughout my entire life.

I know it caused resentment from my brothers, who were too young and thus unaware to understand the dynamics and the why behind everything; they just felt I was more liked, which was untrue. I was just more willing to meet my parents' needs at the detriment of my own.

From this role, I learned I can get a bit of what I need if I give others what they need. For most of my life, I saw this as being kind, but I now realize it is just subconscious manipulation, which was very hard for me to face. Subconsciously, my giving was to get. This didn't align with the "good girl" I needed to believe I was.

Chapter 4

My parents thought building a house would solve all the problems. What they didn't understand is that we actually needed a home.

✺

MY PARENTS FINALLY settled on a house, and in their wisdom, they built a house ten miles away from the closest city. This later became an enormous obstacle when I needed to stay after school for sports or needed a job.

So, the car rides continued each weekend while the house was being built, though the anticipation of a brand new house seemed to lighten my parents' moods, so we weren't complaining. In retrospect, I think their egos were being sufficiently elevated since they could tell everyone they were building a new house, which everyone coveted. We could only see their moods improving, and eventually, we all bought into the "new house, new family, new life" theory.

The house was finally ready to move into, and by now, we were all super excited. I was the only daughter, so I had my own room, complete with a canopy bed. David got his own room as the oldest boy, while my other two brothers shared a room.

Everything in the house was so new and so hopeful. We really believed our lives were changing for the better, that the ugly past was behind us, that our family was now a family of hope, happiness, and maybe even Love. The first night, we ate a picnic on the floor, "grinders," as we called subs in those days, and pizza. For the first time I could remember, I actually felt happy.

Sadly, it didn't last long. Before long, it became obvious that my parents not only overbought for their budget, but after a few rainfalls, the basement flooded. It seems the bad luck found us after all. The rubber band was stretching really far with hope and optimism, and it wasn't long before it snapped right back where it began. Hopelessness, bitterness, and victimhood were never too far away.

As was typical, my parents never really did any due diligence about the builder who lived at the only other house on our street and who really wasn't actually a builder. This was his first foray into building a house, and apparently, he didn't consider the ramifications of building on a downward-sloping wet lot. Unfortunately, my parents didn't either.

As time wore on, a lawsuit had to be filed. After many years, our neighbor filed for bankruptcy, and the water problem never went away. My parents ignored the problem, as they did with every other problem, instead of trying to fix it, and our basement was either dry and smelled of mildew, or in particularly bad rainy seasons, you might find my younger brothers rowing their blow-up floats through the basement.

It never occurred to my parents that a new house would only remain newish if you maintained it. Over the years, the new home became an old wreck and worn out, not unlike its inhabitants.

✹ ✹ ✹

When parents fail to teach a child that finding self-love and feeling safe come from within, the child will spend the rest of their life trying to scavenge for love and safety from the outside.

Fortunately, not all lessons from a dysfunctional childhood are bad. From my parents' poor decision-making, I learned to cross my t's and dot my i's. I am optimistic by nature, but I always look at the worst-case scenario before deciding and look at the consequences way down the line and how they affect everyone, not just me. I have witnessed a new home literally fall apart around me, so I am acutely aware of home maintenance and neglect nothing that requires work.

My parents never attempted to fix anything, including themselves, always taking the approach that they can't. As I matured, I learned that their "I can't" was really an "I won't" and since my first home at 23, an attempt at creating my sense of safety, I never shied away from fixing anything; my goal has been and will probably always be to strive to be the exact opposite of my parents.

The lesson here was that my parents never taught me how to be a mature adult, but they certainly taught me how not to be. It's just sad that I had to miss out on my childhood to get here.

Over the years, the street we lived on filled up, and I can only imagine what the neighbors thought. As my parents realized that the new house would not create a new life, they settled into their old life with a vengeance. Drinking became a nightly occurrence, and all-out screaming matches went right along with it.

It was excruciating being a kid, riding your bike after dinner, and hearing your parents screaming, yelling, and swearing all over the neighborhood. Neighbors raised their kids well, and they never said a word to us, which I am still grateful for to this day. Even in winter, with the windows sealed shut, the house was so poorly made that you could hear the screaming ten houses away.

Worse, when things escalated to throwing things and physical violence, hearing plates smashed was very traumatizing. I literally lived in a war zone my entire childhood.

The house became a metaphor for our lives: as it fell apart, so did our family. Today, children's services would be called, kids placed in foster homes, parents arrested for domestic violence and/or disorderly conduct and child neglect, sent to jail and rehab, and then forced to take parenting classes to get their kids back.

Back then, people deemed it, as my friend Rosalie likes to say, "Not my monkey, not my zoo," and we were on our own. For most of my childhood until high school, when I clearly saw my reality and a way out soon, while other kids were praying for their parents to stay together, I would pray for them to divorce.

※ ※ ※

One of the greatest life lessons my parents taught me is to live the opposite way they lived.

By then, I was well into middle school and trying to get attention in any way I could. I always had a boyfriend, learning early from the false belief that Love needed to come from the outside. Most of these boyfriends did not know what they were dealing with since everything that happened to me stayed in the vault.

The teachers saw my intelligence, and they moved me to the "smart" classes, as they were called back then. Because I was so much ahead of my peers in emotional empathy, logical thinking, and street smarts, I was always a favorite among most adults. This continued my codependent behavior, though at that point, I was so unconscious, I was just happy to have someone value me.

I'm fairly certain that, since we lived so far from town, most adults had no clue what my home life was like, but it's also possible my unconscious neediness was more noticeable than I realized. Still, no one stepped in to help, and it became clearer by the day that I was on my own. The only person who had my back was me, and nobody wanted to hear about anything but positivity from me.

After years of this behavior, I honestly "forgot" that I even had needs. Surviving was what I did daily; I created a world of my own to escape the craziness of my family. I now realize that this was when I truly lost myself, when my authentic self slipped deeply out of awareness, in favor of the self that everyone else seemed to want instead.

At some point, we all adapted to the dysfunctional way of life in the household. To keep Mother safe from killing herself, I learned I needed to be attentive to her while I wasn't in school. I didn't overtly make that decision. I just was her "friend" since she didn't have any, and this seemed to make her happier.

School would end, and I would come home and complete the house chores with her. I had a good sense of humor and a developed sense of metaphors and puns, and spent afternoons amusing my mother. I did not enjoy this; I considered it my job. Mother seemed to live for the time I gave her. As middle school wore on, I tired of "playing" friend to my mother and became less enthusiastic about spending all my free time helping her be a parent.

During this time, our schools became overcrowded, so the "A" class moved to a different time than the other kids in my grade. Since I was in the "A" class, I went to school at different times than my siblings, which gave my mother more access to her playmate. Mother would take me on outings to the mall, as if we were best friends, then take me to lunch before dropping me off at school.

To say I loathed these jaunts is a huge understatement. I knew even then that I was being manipulated for Mother's good, and it felt wrong on so many levels. The pressure to entertain her was intense lest she lash out. I loved Mother, but I also feared her since she held all the power.

Father, up to this point, was a tiny player in our lives. He went to work, came home, ate dinner, drank, and went to bed. Rinse, repeat. I don't recall him ever having anything to say about anything. He lived more like an automaton, a living robot going through the motions of life.

Mother, though severely emotionally immature and lacking in parenting skills, had an innate curiosity about life, even if it was self-centered. By now, I had developed an opinion that Mother was the villain in the horror story of our life, and Father was the victim who would be decent if he had a different wife.

I later learned that they were both the villain and the victim, and Father's mask was much worse than my mother's biting words. Mostly, the final synopsis of my parents' marriage is that the one thing they seemed to have in common was that they both despised each other.

Chapter 5

*Staying as busy as possible to stay
ahead of my thoughts and emotions was
my childhood survival strategy.*

❉

I WAS ALWAYS A high-energy kid, and even in my toxic living situation, I tried to take part in every activity possible. I was a cheerleader and belonged to clubs, sports, Girl Scouts, and anything I could do to get out from under Mother's control. By now, I was doing everything to minimize the after-school time with Mother, and she did not like it.

Mother constantly placed obstacles in my path, so I couldn't do the things I wanted to do. The more she did this, the more resentful I became and the meaner she became—a vicious cycle. Up to this point, I had never asked for anything, whether it was extra money for a mandatory classroom newspaper. Although it was embarrassing, I opted to share a classmate's instead; it was easier than asking or voicing my feelings. The more resentful I became, the meaner Mother was, and the more I tried to assert my boundaries, although back then I didn't realize that's what I was doing.

One particular afternoon stands out vividly. I came home from school, and Mother was on the warpath. Mother wouldn't let me leave until I had folded and put away all the laundry, which was six plus loads. Finally, I snapped and had enough. I told Mother I was tired of doing her job, and at the very least, my brothers should have to help too.

Mother went into a rage. It was not the first time I had witnessed this, but the first time it was specifically directed at me. Mother called me everything she could think of to hurt me, and she dredged up something that had happened when I was five.

While living in Mystic, a family became my surrogate family. The mom, Viola, never had a daughter, and always fixed my unruly curly hair since my mother never did. She taught me how to write my name and to read by the time I was four years old, and essentially loved me when my family didn't. Viola had a younger son, Mark, who was the same age as me, and we were inseparable.

One summer, I was playing over at Mark's house, and he had the idea that we should go into the doghouse and play "I'll show you mine if you show me yours." I was a fairly clueless little kid in that regard, and said okay. Once I realized what he meant, I bolted, crying, and told Viola.

I begged her not to tell Mother since I was so terrified that Mother would blame and punish me. I assumed Viola kept her promise. Fast forward to the fateful day when I finally asserted myself with Mother. When she realized I wasn't buckling, she threw in my face the situation with Mark seven years earlier.

Mother deliberately shamed me, and it was then that I really saw her viciousness. This one act of meanness became a foundation for how I viewed Love: people who Love you will hurt you. It never occurred to me up to this point that Mother had her own issues, as well as being abusive, and the behavior was completely unacceptable.

From this point on, Mother had crossed a line, and the damage was irreparable. I still loved her and went through the motions, but I knew she was emotionally unsafe. Emotional walls became more reinforced, and I did virtually anything to get out of the house. One of those activities was Girl Scouts, which met on Monday evenings in town. Mother was usually too drunk by then or deliberately making it difficult for me, so Father had to take me.

At first, he seemed to be a better choice, and at least he wasn't mean to me, and since he never talked, it was actually quite peaceful, that is, until he started making sexual advances. Nothing seemed to shock me, and I did everything in my power to stay as far away from him as he drove.

The problem was that he was an adult who had the power, and eventually, he would touch me inappropriately. What started in the car now extended to the house, and from then on, I spent a lot of emotional and physical energy trying to avoid him. He started making suggestive comments about my looks or development that disgusted me, but I tried to ignore them.

One time, I was doing just that, and I went into the basement rec room, which was dark. He grabbed me. He had been drinking, and he said all kinds of horrible sexual things. At first, I froze, but eventually, I got up the courage to break away and lock myself in my room. That was the last day I attended Girl Scouts.

What's sad is that at no point did I ever consider telling anyone. I was conditioned by now to believe that Father was a good person because he worked hard every day to pay the bills, and I felt that saying anything would only ruin any type of stability my younger brothers had with him.

My older brother was not a consideration because, by now, being the scapegoat, he hated Father anyhow. Telling Mother was not an option since, after she shamed me about something that took place when I was five, I believed this would just give her more ammunition for later use. Besides, I knew without a doubt she wouldn't care.

Literally, from that point on, I did everything in my power to avoid Father. He was essentially emotionally void and lacking in any communication skills, so this wasn't all that difficult. If there were ever an activity that required me to be alone with him, I would just quit or not attend.

Mother was so caught up in her own little world that she either didn't notice or didn't care. Mostly, I put this behind me and moved on. It wasn't until adulthood and many difficult intimate relationships that I realized I never put it behind me, but buried it with all my other secrets and shame, reliving the shame in each toxic relationship choice.

A monumental event that stands out was when I was around thirteen, when Mother announced that Father had something very important to tell me and David. I was literally thrilled and relieved; finally, my parents would answer my prayers. My parents were divorcing! My relief was tremendous!

This was a very plausible conclusion since Mother had violated her own self-imposed guideline of not drinking before 5 p.m., and by the time we arrived home from school, she was plastered. Nothing abnormal. Father was drunk as well.

Father shepherded my brother and me into my brother's bedroom. The door shut loudly, and Father said he had something to tell us. Relief is what I felt until he blurted out, "I am not your real father." I can't tell you how disappointed I was by this news, not because it made me sad, but I was so hopeful that my parents were divorcing.

Regarding the news itself, I can honestly say I felt nothing. There was no room for asking questions or exploring our emotional responses. In fact, after that one sentence, we were "dismissed" with the unspoken understanding that we were never to ask questions. For me, it's sad to say, but it both made sense, and I felt a sense of relief as I absorbed the news.

Father, actually, Stepfather, seemed completely emotionless, literally like he was an empty shell of a person—no passions, no curiosity, no opinions. Today, I would say he was like a computer that was missing its software.

After the big reveal, Mother got it in her drunken head to take me to the mall. The thing that really stood out above everything that night was what a miracle it was that we survived as drunk as she was swerving in and out of lanes, a clear message even then that we really have guardian angels looking out for us.

The conversation with Stepfather went into the vault, where it stayed most of my life.

✻ ✻ ✻

> *I often ask myself, what's more damaging: a mother who was mean all the time or a mother who was mean most of the time and kind sometimes?*

As middle school ended, once again, we all adapted. I continued to avoid Stepfather, which was easy since he avoided us, and Mother continued to push and pull on my emotions. My family became a battleground of manipulation to see who got their needs met and who didn't.

What's really interesting is that there were moments of kindness in my family, mostly from Mother. In retrospect, this caused more damage than good because it was easier for me, emotionally as a kid, just to keep my guard up than drop it and have my heart broken over and over. It also sets the stage for abusive romantic relationships decades later, where I would tolerate verbal abuse, an apology or gift offered, and I would accept this as "normal"; after all, it felt so familiar.

As an example of Mother's sporadic kindness, I was in love with David Cassidy. Mother somehow knew this and bought tickets for the entire family to see him in concert, even taking the time to style my hair before we went, which she never did. She also purchased tickets for the family to see the New England Patriots, which was David's favorite sports team.

On weekends when Stepfather was sleeping and we all had to tiptoe around the house for fear of waking him, Mother would take us on "nature hikes" in the woods around our home. In my senior year in high school, Mother decided to take us to Disney. What's incredible is that none of us wanted to go. Other than Bruce, who was too young to decide, we all stayed home to fend for ourselves.

I believe there were moments of caring from Mother; however, the inconsistency really messed with my head. As an adult, I have tolerated ill treatment because I learned firsthand that hurt people who claim to love you hurt you, and this seemed "normal" to me.

Unhealthy relationships felt "familiar and normal." Despite the random acts of kindness from my mother, I never did fully trust her, ever. I knew she harbored a very vindictive, bitter side, and truthfully, I was always on guard during the "nature hikes," wondering if her actual intent was to leave us behind or worse.

Chapter 6

If you bury your pain deeply enough, at some point, you can fool yourself into thinking you are actually happy and whole.

✺

HIGH SCHOOL ARRIVED, and this marked the beginning of my love for sports. To this day, I'm not entirely sure if I loved sports or if I loved the attention it gave me. In my freshman year, I played basketball and was quite good at it, as I was eager to please, even though I had never watched a basketball game in my life.

Growing up where we did, the TV signal limited us to three TV channels. The main TV was where my parents were, so I opted to read instead. I read book after book as a kid, and I owe a lot of my intelligence, emotional resilience, and awareness to the escape the books provided. To this day, I rarely watch TV; it's a habit I never adopted.

While playing sports my freshman year, my basketball coach noticed my running ability and suggested that I try track in the spring. Again, I had no emotional connection to this but did so to please the coach, who seemed interested in me.

It turns out I wasn't just good at running; I was great. Partly because of genetics, but mostly because of my need to win at all costs. I was not afraid to work hard, always willing to work harder and longer than my peers, and soon running became "my thing."

Before long, I was beating everyone on my team, then everyone else as well. Losing became a "non" option, and, as I later learned in therapy, I was running from my home life and demons, and this made me unbeatable. By sophomore year, I was breaking every running record in cross country. I had become a superstar runner overnight.

What was so sad is that I could never enjoy it. Every race, I had to do better, and it was never enough. Zero support came from my family. At this point in my life, I was 100 percent on my own. I can never recall my parents asking about school, homework, grades, friends, or accomplishments, and they never attended one track or cross-country meet.

The only time Mother went to a track meet, she stayed in the car reading *The National Enquirer*; I won four races that day. I didn't care so much that she didn't watch. I expected that, but it embarrassed me. She made a display of how little I meant to her—more shame in the vault.

I was in the papers all the time, and it heralded me as the girl to beat—each accomplishment I internalized. I never talked about it. I just ran my races and won. Rinse, repeat. Looking back, this is when Mother really resented me.

High school allowed me to branch out more, and I seized the opportunity full-on. The more I accomplished, the more I experienced Mother's jealousy. I later confirmed this in many mediumship readings after Mother passed, as well as from Mother's sister. Finally, I felt validated, and it actually felt good to confirm what I thought to be true but had no way to prove.

Mother could never conceptualize that my accomplishments were because of my hard work, instead deeming me "lucky" and, in her own bitterness, doing practically everything she could to undermine me. It was not unusual to win a tournament with 500 runners, come home, and have Mother completely ignore me.

David was the only family member who consistently showed any interest and would watch my races when he wasn't playing his sports; my other two brothers were less aware because of their age.

Strangers started befriending me. Runners, parents, and coaches became my emotional base. As far as I knew, everyone was oblivious to my parents' drinking and home life, though I could be mistaken since they were now full-blown alcoholics.

Getting rides home from sports and activities became a chore, and I would wait for a ride because of Mother's passive-aggressive manner for an hour or two, or more. Yet, I couldn't complain for fear it would be worse the next day. So I swallowed my anger, knowing that if I expressed myself, I might have to quit sports, which were saving my life, even if I didn't overtly realize it.

❈ ❈ ❈

When you "inherit" your reaction to your parents' faulty thinking and programming, it often takes a lifetime to undo it.

Mother had a lot of challenging traits, but one that really stood out was her need to rank people above or below herself. Because Mother was an alcoholic and very malnourished, she was always belittling heavier women, and this was another legacy she left me with.

As a runner, I was always fit, but not necessarily waif-like. Mother was always gloating about how thin she was, and I'm sure it was a way for her to make me feel less than (at this point in my life, I did not understand that no one can make me feel anything) and attempt to feel better than me in something.

I often felt the hypocrisy of Mother's weight—she was thin because she was incredibly unhealthy. This sparked a lifelong commitment to a plant-based diet and a greater awareness of health on all levels. As running became a cornerstone of my life and boys became more important, my weight became a focal point. It was during a sleepover in seventh grade that a friend explained how she ate and then threw up, which helped her control her weight. I filed this away for future use.

By sophomore year, I was hyper-focused on my weight. What clinched it was when a boy at school made a passing remark about my butt that I really took action. I started starving myself, and then I had a five-inch growth spurt; I became tall and super thin.

Everyone noticed that I was an even better runner, and this fed the demon well. The stress of my home and actual hunger often made me binge, and I pulled out my seventh-grade story, and purging became part of the repertoire. I didn't rely on this; I didn't have to, since my self-discipline was quite strong. But it was nice to know I had a tool I could use when needed. Of course, no one noticed.

By mid-high school, I had achieved a weight of 105 pounds, all muscle at 5'6", and this lasted for most of college. Looking back, I'm certain I looked emaciated, but like everything else, no one questioned it. I'm guessing Mother wasn't happy either.

To this day, I still have a very distorted view of my weight, never seeing reality on my 5'6", 115-pound muscular frame; I still feel "huge" most days, though I have mostly learned to accept myself. After all, it's only the cover of the book, not the book itself. Childhood damage is very pervasive and lingering.

Besides sports, I was an excellent student and managed life as well as expected. Because doors into other people's lives were being opened, I thought about "getting out."

As a survival strategy, I never allowed myself to dwell on how awful my home life was because I didn't want to take on the negative emotions of my parents: hate, bitterness, blame, victimhood, self-centeredness, lack of gratitude, and helplessness. My ability to block emotions made this easier.

Because of this awareness, I strived to be the exact opposite: optimistic, disciplined, loving, selfless, and full of gratitude. Many of these qualities I had were innate, and others I learned. I knew if I wanted to achieve something, I could as long as I put in the effort. The more positive and successful I became, the nastier Mother became. I still feared her, but mostly just had her on "ignore." I learned I could get support elsewhere, and that's what I did.

Chapter 7

*Hiding the family secrets and burying
the shame became a full-time job.*

✺

DURING MY SOPHOMORE year, I started dating a boy. This relationship lasted five years, culminating in an engagement that I ended. I was deeply in love for all five years until the very last day.

He was from one of the more prominent families in town, and the fact that he liked me validated that I wasn't the bad person I unconsciously felt I was. His parents were kind to me, but because I came from such a "bad" family, I gave him everything, took nothing, and didn't ask for anything either.

Looking back, I was so ashamed of my family. I felt unworthy of him in my life, and I completely subordinated myself to every need he had. I felt inferior in every way and had him on an impossibly high pedestal. He loved the arrangement. Looking back, this was my first toxic relationship. Though I was so needy and blind, I was completely unaware of how bad it was.

One situation that really stands out was the summer of my junior year. My parents started drinking early on this particular

Saturday, and instead of passing out, which was the norm, things just kept escalating until they were physically assaulting one another and violently trashing the house.

Eventually, things got so bad that one of my brothers called the police, and they were both arrested. By now, it was 3 a.m. My brother and I spent the next several hours cleaning until my boyfriend picked me up to go to a professional baseball game with his family. My brother was livid, rightfully so, because I was leaving it to him to finish "fixing" everything, but I was so ashamed of the situation and couldn't think of a way to get out of going, since they had already purchased the ticket. I mentioned none of this to my boyfriend.

About a week later, he called me, furious. I had embarrassed him by not telling him about the arrest (it was in the local paper), and his family wanted to know what happened; it blindsided him. He never asked about me, my feelings, how I had coped, etc. Absolutely zero empathy; I felt little and took on his anger, which led me to believe I brought this on myself. This was the first relationship where a significant lack of empathy was evident, a trend that continued in every subsequent romantic relationship until recently.

Again, more shame in the vault. At this point, I was praying this was the end of the family craziness, that maybe even my parents would realize it had gone too far. Unfortunately, that was not the case.

❋ ❋ ❋

When life appeared as though it couldn't possibly get any worse, somehow, my parents found a way to make it so.

Mother and Stepfather's alcoholism spiraled further out of control. Mother began taking antidepressants, presumably without the doctor knowing she was an alcoholic. So now, she would drink, take her medication, and blackout until morning.

How she didn't overdose is beyond me, but truthfully, we weren't all that worried. It was the only time in years and years when things were actually quiet at night. The normal routine was that Mother would start drinking at 5 p.m., Stepfather would come home drunk, and they would scream and yell all night until they both passed out.

I was very disciplined by this time and knew I needed enough sleep to function the next day. I would attempt to go to bed by 9:30 and, if lucky, things might quiet down by 11. This was an enormous source of resentment for me, but I couldn't say a word. On those occasions I did, I would get sucked into their battles, so I tried to keep my mouth shut as much as possible.

The typical arguments with my parents centered around Mother screaming for some sort of response from Stepfather, and Stepfather remaining emotionally disconnected. It was for this reason that, for most of my life, I felt that Mother was the biggest perpetrator, since Stepfather seemed less antagonistic.

Not until I got into similar relationships did I understand the frustration of being with someone emotionally unavailable, and I finally understood that silence and stonewalling can be a form of emotional abuse.

If the night was more volatile than typical, Mother might try to reach out to David and me for attention, especially if she was feeling frustrated or attention-seeking from Stepfather's lack of response. This never worked because by now, we were sick of the whole thing and didn't want to play.

Mother was much more manipulative than we gave her credit for, so what she started doing was threatening to kill herself. With the imprint from early childhood, this got our attention. For most of high school, she would periodically sit at the table completely drunk with a large butcher knife in front of her, essentially holding David and me hostage so she wouldn't kill herself. This could go on for hours, and the next day, we would get up for school as if it had never happened. More shame stuffed in the vault of shame. Rinse, repeat.

I feel terrible saying this, but at some point, I lost the will to care. It had gotten to the point where I was so beaten down emotionally that I just didn't care anymore if she killed herself or not. I still loved her deeply, but the emotional torment was just too much to handle. To this day, I can't say for sure if she ever knew half of the torture she put us through as kids.

My brother, Kenny, told a story about twenty years ago, when they were at a family picnic, and Mother told him she had been an exemplary mother. Kenny didn't let it slide since he had become a single parent to my niece when my niece's mother misused substances, knowing how pitiful a mother she actually was. Kenny recalls Mother looking at him in disbelief. Denial is an unbelievable defense mechanism, and Mother had it mastered.

Many of the conflicting emotions I carried about Mother were another source of shame. After all, what dutiful daughter doesn't care if her mother takes her life? I now know it was simply a response to years of emotional abuse, and I was at my breaking point; who could have done better? I did the best I could under the circumstances.

Chapter 8

*The biggest shock is when you realize you've spent
your entire childhood trying to fill your cup from
the outside, but not realizing the cup had holes.*

✹

HIGH SCHOOL CONTINUED, and I accumulated more and more awards and accolades. I spent every free minute with my boyfriend and his family. Mother had an outright disdain for my boyfriend and family, presumably because it highlighted how poorly she felt about herself and her situation. I was fully aware of Mother's animosity toward me and did everything to minimize it.

In every childhood, I believe certain events cause a shift. One of these events happened when I was a sophomore. Since I started school at four years old, most assumed I was a year older based on my grade, so my boyfriend assumed I was a year older. I never corrected this; however, the time came to drive, and obviously, I couldn't.

I got myself caught in a pickle because my boyfriend wanted me to visit him at college, which was 50 miles away, and I didn't know how to say I couldn't and disappoint him.

So, I got the foolish idea of taking the car while my brother played football, intending to have it back by the end of the game. The plan was good; the execution was terrible.

The car was a manual, which I had never driven, yet this didn't stop me. At this point, I had the belief I was capable of anything. I drove the car to see my boyfriend; however, on the way back, the engine caught on fire, and that's when things went downhill fast. I got a ride from a very kind man to a town not too far from home, called my parents, and literally, Mother went crazy, even crazy for her.

Looking back, I was her shining star, proof that the family wasn't as bad as it was, a source of her self-esteem, even though she never let on to me. Now, Mother hated me as this incident somehow caused an injury to her ego that was unparalleled. Mother literally destroyed every single thing in my room, and all I could do was stand back and watch. Stepfather, as an extreme avoidant, did nothing.

For two days, I went unfed and ignored. I still went to school as if nothing had happened, still excelled, but I developed a hatred for Mother that was deeply embedded, which added to my deep belief that I was a "bad girl." That summer, I worked three jobs and paid it all back, but I was now treated as if I were the scum of the earth.

What's really interesting about this story is what I thought about it as it was happening. I was fully aware of the dynamic of what was taking place without having the medical terms for Mother's disorder, and I also knew that this was probably the best thing for me in the long run.

My ego was getting too big, and on some level, I felt grateful that it hadn't gotten out of control. I believe that had this not happened, my life would have gone much differently, and it's possible that I would have eventually adopted the negative qualities of my parents, being a taker rather than a giver, which is really my true essence.

The relationship with Mother was already lacking. This made me realize I needed to get away from her to survive. I became more focused on school, running, student council, yearbook, and anything else I could find to offset how I felt about myself and my family.

✹ ✹ ✹

It's sad when my closest companions growing up were emotional betrayal and neglect.

As far back as I can recall, Mother ignored anything that was of any value to me. I won creative writing contests and many other school contests, not a word. Sports successes, not a word. Academic awards, not a word. Homecoming queen, this she noticed.

In my senior year, they nominated me for homecoming queen, and we did it differently. Typically, the nomination process is purely a popularity contest. Although it was still to some extent, people could donate money—a penny per vote—which went toward funding the homecoming dance. Whoever had the most money would win. The contest appealed to me, and I was determined to win. My self-esteem could not fathom losing, so I did everything to win.

My boyfriend's sister was in my class, and since his family was quite wealthy, they also contributed, and I won. The overriding emotion upon being crowned the winner was "Oh, no! I don't want to be the homecoming queen!" The truth is, I just wanted to win. The title meant nothing to me; my shaky self-esteem "needed" to win.

I had grown up in a new home that was simply a mask for a dysfunctional family, and homecoming queen seemed so not me; on some level, I felt unworthy. There was an entire weekend of activities, and I couldn't wait for it all to be over.

I even wondered if I could give the crown to someone more "suitable."

What really hit hard, though, was Mother's reaction. After never having gone to a race or academic achievement event, Mother and Stepfather couldn't wait to go to the football game to see me honored as "Queen." This bothered me so much, and it really made it that much more of a farce to partake in the weekend. After all that had happened in my life, ironically, it is a weekend I consider one of my worst.

I learned a great lesson about winning at all costs. I also never saw this as a negative for anyone who wanted to be crowned homecoming queen. It just wasn't for me. I had a similar experience with high school cheerleading, a role which everyone coveted. Again, just to win, I tried out. I made the team, and then I immediately realized there was no way I could cheer for anyone in the same sports I excelled in. I'm guessing my mother would have watched me cheer had I accepted the position.

※ ※ ※

Sometimes, the more someone tries to push you down, the more you rise above. The problem is distinguishing between this as "true" self-esteem versus one's ego trying to survive.

Running became my savior, and I continued to rack up awards. My parents still ignored me and offered no support or congratulations, which made me feel internally proud of myself, rather than looking outside for recognition. Sadly, it also made me feel like I didn't need anyone, and this was something that took a lifetime to overcome, especially since I didn't even realize it was a problem. I was actually proud of being so self-sufficient and loving to everyone else, just not to myself, not that I was consciously aware of this.

My senior year rolled in, and I was determined to go to college. I signed up for the SAT myself, got a ride, received the results, and was featured in many *Who's Who* publications. I was also ultra-focused on figuring out how I was going to pay.

My parents never went to college and, probably not a surprise, never considered this as an option for my brothers and me. They never asked, and I just kept my dreams to myself. I was getting piles of mail every day from colleges trying to recruit me for running, but with no guidance, I didn't know what it meant in terms of opportunities and scholarships.

My goal at this point was to attend college close to my boyfriend and close to home, since I was at the beginning stages of survivor's guilt, knowing I would get out, and my brothers probably wouldn't. I chose a college that offered some scholarship money (I'm sure I could have gotten a full ride somewhere had I been aware), and I set out to figure out how to afford the rest.

On my own I learned I needed to apply for financial aid, so I figured out how much and when I needed their current tax returns and my parents were thwarting my every effort to get out, I completed their tax returns for them, filed them, emancipated myself from my family, and got enough money to go to college.

It was so shocking that it worked out that it wasn't until they dropped me off at my dorm that I finally felt like I could breathe. I felt blessed to have the resilience and determination to find my way out of such a chaotic environment.

My entire family dropped me off, which seemed so confusing since we never did anything as a "family." The only thing my mother could say was how sorry she felt for me because the room was so small. I'm sure her reaction was to offset her own sense of inferiority. What she couldn't understand was that I would have gladly lived in a closet just to get out from under her.

And so I got out. Survivor's guilt was tremendous, and this is where my need to help my brothers went into full gear and lasted until recently. I felt blessed to have survived and to have the resilience and self-efficacy to help myself and my situation.

I was in heaven to go to classes, run, do homework, and not have to listen to fighting and suicide threats every night. I worked all during college and wrote for the school paper, which I loved. My genuine passion was journalism, but I chose finance because I was aware that I was 100 percent on my own, and this offered a "safer" future.

Still, the family problems followed me. It wasn't unusual for my brothers to call me asking for help to navigate the violence they were in, and I felt so bad and guilty that I wasn't a part of it anymore.

I rarely came home, and my parents never called me during the four years I was away at college. In fact, they never called me in my entire adult life, except to ask for something, typically money. I was so used to neglect that this seemed normal to me. Considered way more mature for my age, I really struggled to relate to the rest of my peers, who complained about going to class while I was grateful for being out of the war zone.

I became the go-to person if someone had a problem, and I still never said a word about myself. I was finally content, though looking back, I was living with PTSD and did not know it. From my perspective, it was adrenaline, and it propelled me to continue moving forward successfully. I spent most of my free time at my boyfriend's school and never took part in typical college activities. I honestly couldn't relate, and I'm sure I was a puzzle to most.

When sophomore year in college rolled around, I moved off campus with a running teammate. My mother gave me a box of food, which was her way of saying she wasn't expecting me back home. Still, I came home most weekends to work, so the usual routine was I would drive home with my boyfriend late Saturday night, sleep at my parents' house, get up before the family, go to work, and return to college.

Most weekends, I never saw my family at all, and I despised spending the night at home for several reasons. First, going home brought up all the stress and negative memories I had experienced growing up. Since everything was in the vault and my chief aim with my boyfriend was to give the sense we were normal, I kept this to myself, which made it worse.

Second, somewhere in high school, Mother decided it would be a bright idea if she got her own dog since Jumbo had allegiance to Stepfather. So Mother got a chihuahua and aptly named him Muchacho. Muchacho became a source of considerable contempt within the family for several reasons.

From my brothers' perspective, which was not untrue, Mother treated Muchacho much more lovingly than all of us combined. Mother's neglectfulness was far-reaching. For example, even though Stepfather had top-of-the-line health and dental insurance, one had to be dying to get any type of treatment. This was pure laziness and a general lack of concern since back then, there were no copays. I was less resentful since I was so independent. I took it upon myself to manage my healthcare. My parents' neglect of our healthcare early on has been a huge contributing factor to my brother's lifelong, unnecessary dental problems.

Muchacho was a different story. The dog might have been small, but he certainly was mighty, possibly the only one to get his needs met. Muchacho was always getting into things because, like her kids, Mother never kept a watch, and the dog could do anything.

At one point, Muchacho needed a very expensive kidney surgery with a promise of fifty-fifty success, and Mother was all in; we all debated whether she would have done the same for her kids. We still can't be sure.

My biggest issue wasn't this, though. On the one hand, Mother was very tidy; on the other hand, she was not clean. Muchacho would poop and pee anywhere, and because the house carpet was dark green, Mother would simply pick up the poop and call it a day. There was no sterilizing or cleaning of the carpet, and I found this to be absolutely abhorrent.

Worse to me was that the dog's favorite spot to pee was in my bedroom on my canopy dust ruffle. It was amazing to me that Mother never even questioned why the dog didn't pee, or maybe she knew, and this was her passive-aggressive way of getting back at me.

By now, I knew Mother harbored massive resentment and jealousy toward me, and I made sure I minimized all accomplishments. I was still excelling at school and running, but they never asked. I never told. I got into the practice of only bringing up the "bad things," sometimes even making them up, because it made them happy, learning performance over presence.

✳ ✳ ✳

I was 20 going on 40. Someone forgot to mention that life at 20 was supposed to be fun.

At 20, I realized I needed to earn more money than I made at my weekend job, so I applied for a manager's position at an athletic store, and they hired me. My starting salary was $360 a week, a large sum back then, and I somehow managed to run the store, attend classes, write for the school paper, and still find time to run.

My parents did not know about anything going on in my life, so I just accepted that I was on my own. I had become so independent and self-sufficient that nothing bothered me. I had essentially shut down negative feelings or emotional needs and just did whatever was necessary to get by. Survival was my motto as I kept anything and everything negative and shameful in the vault out of awareness.

During the first year in my college apartment, I was walking back from class, and a man called me over to his car. I walked over, only to discover that he was exposing himself to me. I calmly walked away, unemotionally told my roommates, and called the police. The police, in their wisdom, brought the man to our apartment to identify him.

After I did, the police asked me to go to the police station to complete the paperwork. I first had to stop by my class and let the professor, who had a strict attendance policy, know why I wouldn't be in class.

When I called her into the hall to tell her, she both cried and hugged me; I remember being mystified by her emotional reaction. I had experienced so many violations up to this point that I barely blinked an eye over this experience and wondered why the fuss. My concern was for other young girls who might have a similar experience and not be as tough as I was.

That following summer, I was staying at the apartment by myself and received a call at midnight from a man saying that he knew I was alone, and that he was going to come and kill me. I actually never made the connection until this minute. That might have been the flasher, though either way, I called the police, and they said there was nothing they could do. That night, I slept on the couch with a view of the front door, with a butcher knife next to me, with the thought that I would be ready if someone came in.

I told no one. I just handled it myself.

Chapter 9

Hiding from my truth was exhausting and made my daily 10-mile runs seem like nothing.

❋

WHEN I WAS a sophomore in college and my boyfriend was a senior, his family went on a cross-country road trip, and they invited me. My parents couldn't care less, though I had to make a big show for my boyfriend's family, explaining that I asked and my family said OK. I can't recall even asking. At this point, I was completely on my own, physically, emotionally, and financially, which I'm sure no one realized, given the vault's tight seal.

Two years prior, during my senior year in high school, Mother developed severe pancreatitis, and though nobody explained this, my brothers and I acknowledged it was from drinking. Mother was in and out of the hospital that entire year, so there were periods of relief from the constant yelling. However, I needed to stay vigilant because Stepfather had full access to me. In retrospect, I think he became deathly afraid of me, knowing I would take none of his crap, so he largely stayed away. Again, this was all kept to myself, even though I spent enormous amounts of time with my boyfriend and his family.

Summer came, and we embarked on the two-week-long road trip. I had to give the illusion that my family was "normal," so I would make calls home. These calls were both excruciating and anxiety-filled because I had to make believe they were happy I called and not resentful that I was away on vacation.

On one such call, I found out Mother had almost died with her most recent bout of pancreatitis. Turns out, they gave her a stern talking to that she could never drink again, which Mother ignored. This time, the pancreas had become so damaged that she had gone into shock, and she needed to have a Whipple procedure, a surgery so new in those days that she could have died on the table. Sadly, I felt nothing but put on a show of great concern, an Academy Award in lying.

I felt bad that I didn't care, but it really wasn't that as much as the fact that I had to resign myself early on to the fact that Mother was probably going to die either by suicide or drinking herself to death, which was just another form of suicide from my perspective.

If there was an emotion I felt, it was resentment, which I know sounds callous. I was angry that Mother was messing up my trip, and truthfully, I had an attitude of "it figures Mother would do this."

Mother loved being sick. In desperate need of attention, being ill, she got plenty of it. Before understanding alcoholism as a disease, I always wondered if she deliberately ignored the doctor's warnings and got sick for attention and to avoid the monotony of her life. I didn't end up having to cut my trip short, but it added to my anxiety, always fearful that they would figure out my charade and that I would be unworthy of my boyfriend's love and family.

Mother finally had the Whipple procedure at the only hospital that was doing them at the time, sixty miles away, and I think the doctors finally caught on at this more advanced hospital to the extent of her alcoholism. They again gave her the edict never to drink again, and even without drinking, the Whipple would only extend her life for twenty years if Mother did what she was told. My mother never quit drinking, somehow beating the odds and living another twenty-four years. Truly a medical mystery, it's sad she never saw the miracle or the gift.

Also, during my sophomore year at college, my boyfriend proposed to me. Honestly, this stressed me out as well because there was this expectation that my parents felt overjoyed, like everyone else's parents, and I knew this wasn't true. Personally, I couldn't care less, but I needed to give the impression that I cared and that my family would be ecstatic, just like his would.

It was night by the time I got back and had a phone, and since I knew my parents were drunk or passed out, I made a show of calling and acted as if they weren't home. I got away with it since my boyfriend had no clue what I was dealing with. Keeping my family dynamics away from him was a full-time job, and I was positive that if he knew, he would leave me.

Was I happy to be engaged? It's hard to really say. I think I was happier being validated as worthy of him. He had a pretty sweet deal. I worshiped him and asked for nothing, which is exactly what I got. To me, this felt just like home.

By the time my boyfriend graduated from college, he had gone to law school under the Marines' Juris Doctorate program, and for the first time in five years, we were going to be apart for over five days, in fact, for the entire summer. I was going to work at his family store, which I had done for several previous summers, and he was going to bootcamp.

Initially, I was nervous being alone, but he left me his car to use, and frankly, I didn't miss him all that much. I didn't really consider what this meant since I was so busy. However, something clearly was changing inside me. Then, the shoe dropped. Until this point, I had my boyfriend on a pedestal and thought he was everything I wasn't—strong, well-adjusted, self-assured—but then he got homesick and couldn't handle bootcamp.

Within a few weeks, he "faked" an injury, which his family bought into, though they probably knew the truth, and they involved the Red Cross and had him honorably discharged. Though he came home superfit and physically strong, I knew he was emotionally weak, and I immediately fell out of love with him.

I realized I was ten times stronger, and on a subconscious level, I knew he was a privileged, self-centered little boy who "loved me" because of the attention I gave him and how little he had to do to sustain the relationship. I tried getting the feeling back, and by the end of the summer, I ended the relationship. He had an emotional breakdown over the ending, which solidified what I already knew: I was way too emotionally strong for him, and I was done.

What has since struck me is how low I had set the bar for my needs being met and how much I gave. A few months after the breakup, his new girlfriend came into the store I was managing and told me that my ex-boyfriend had said I was beautiful, and she wanted to see for herself.

During the five years I was with him, he had never mentioned this to me, and it really shocked me. I never made the correlation until much later in life that no one had ever said I was beautiful—not even my parents—which is why I was so surprised. I assumed I was just average at best. It wasn't until decades later that I realized my boyfriend found me beautiful, yet he kept his opinions to himself, much like Mother.

❋ ❋ ❋

Sometimes you don't realize you are drowning when you are too busy trying to keep everyone else afloat.

After the breakup, I regrouped and tried to figure out my life. This was one of the most challenging periods I could remember because I felt I had no anchor. I had a sense of being thrown back and forth, which I did my best to ignore.

I started taking up martial arts after getting involved with a college professor, which was an attempt to find some stability. This was the first person in a line of many that I dated who was an alcoholic, and it didn't last long. I was very aware of the probability of being attracted to an alcoholic, so I tried really hard to avoid this, which ironically didn't work that way.

Shortly after ending my relationship with the professor, I went on a date with someone who owned an electronics store in the mall, and we were together for eight years. My attraction to him was this: he didn't drink, and he didn't require emotional intimacy. In my distorted view, a perfect partner!

This relationship, I always considered as respite care for me. I knew it was seriously lacking in depth, but it was easy, and I needed a break. I never really intended it to last as long as it did; however, the boy was an only child, and his parents loved me, and I loved them. The tradeoff was that I needed to play the role as they needed and cater to their son, something I knew well.

On the surface, we seemed to have a great relationship: we both loved staying fit, we restored apartments, and we basically focused on our careers, living parallel lives. His issue was that he was rather shallow, and since he had never dated, he felt our relationship was the pinnacle; plus, we had an unspoken agreement. I would mother him in exchange for access to his family.

We were financially compatible, so we saved a ton of money. Although I knew much was missing and that I was worlds ahead of him emotionally, I was relatively content living in this fantasy world. He didn't drink, and we never fought. The peace was very nice; plus, I finally got some mothering from his mom, though at the cost of losing myself further. We never talked long-term. Intimacy in any form was nil, but for eight years, it worked. And then it didn't.

I took a job at a local bank, and before long, I met a new commercial lender and fell madly in love. This was the first time I had ever been in love, and with such a barren emotional life, I felt defenseless to the feelings. I would love to say I handled it well, but I didn't, and since my partner and I were well-known in the small town where we lived, it didn't go well.

Looking back, I believe this man came into my path to wake me up, as I was in an emotional fog at the time, and he did just that. The previous relationship ended with both of us feeling like we had lost a good friend; I think his parents lost as much, if not more, than we did.

PANEL TWO

The Stories I Lived

*I became the character,
mistaking the script for truth.*

Chapter 1

*Life continues on autopilot, driving your life forward
until you wake up and realize you were driving
with a dirty windshield and ended up going
in the wrong direction.*

✱

BY THE TIME I was 23 and out of college, I had already managed an athletic store and sold insurance policies. The insurance business was not enjoyable at all, so I set out to find something different. I graduated with a degree in finance (later psychology), which was chosen because I didn't know what else to choose, and I knew my genuine passion, journalism, was a long shot for the financial security I needed.

So, with my typical enthusiasm and never-fail attitude, I landed a sales job in banking and never looked back. The positive aspect of my upbringing was that it never occurred to me I wouldn't be successful, and in sales, that's a very beneficial quality.

What I quickly learned was that making money would be very easy for me. My first banking position in the mid-80s earned me $65,000 in commission, and it never fazed me one bit. I never chased money for material gain—it simply offered a sense of safety I couldn't yet find within myself. I worked hard, had a positive personality, and had tons of energy; I did well.

At my first position, I was lending at a private bank that was the first in the country, and we attracted the wealthiest clients. It exposed me to fine dining, extravagance, and lots of different people. I was still clueless about myself, mostly relying on my effort more than anything.

At one cocktail party, an older woman took me aside and said I was absolutely gorgeous, and again, I remember being completely mystified. Surely she was joking or talking about someone else.

But she wasn't.

I had been so neglected and ignored, I really didn't know how I looked; this often got me in trouble with male clients. As always, I was super friendly, assertive, smart, and ambitious, and the men seemed to love this while I was oblivious to my impact. I often found myself in awkward positions with men trying to grab my attention, delivering flowers to my work, or sending a limo for a business lunch. I just didn't get it. This caused a lot of animosity with the less attractive female lenders at the bank, who thought I was playing a game, not knowing I suffered emotional abuse as a child, and thus, had no clear understanding of myself.

I was making money like crazy and absorbing all the experiences it exposed me to. Survivor's guilt was immense because of the opulent lifestyle I was currently living. Mother had divorced Stepfather after he lost his job because of drinking and smashing the new company truck, and she was crying poverty. Mother was a pro at tugging at my heartstrings.

Giving Mother money became a routine thing to do. Mother was bitter that she had to find a job and took every handout, believing I owed it to her since she had birthed me (her words). I made sure I never told her of my success, but she instinctively knew if she asked for money, she would get it.

Today, having kids of my own, I find it appalling she would ask, and even more so that she would take. This became a family dynamic for everyone. Tricia made money. Tricia is easy to manipulate. Tricia will bail us out, and I did. I morphed into the family bank, and while it was my choice to assume this role, I realize it benefited no one in the long run. We all continued to play our family roles well.

❋ ❋ ❋

Fear is the root of all missteps off our path. It can propel one forward with outward success, but not necessarily in a direction that fills our Soul.

Even if I disliked a position, my competitive nature drove me to excel, and I wouldn't stop at anything to achieve that. Most people had the impression I was driven by money. I never was. That was the furthest from the truth. The recipe was simple—I worked harder than anyone, and the money followed.

To this day, I never spend more than what I have earned because of what I learned in my childhood. I knew I would always be responsible for my life with no fallback, so even at a very young age, I saved like crazy. Fear and lack ruled my life.

In a short period, I developed a name for myself in the real estate mortgage market, and within a year, another company from Texas, which wanted to come into the area, reached out to interview me. I figured, why not? By the end of that week, the company had hired me to start and run a mortgage company; I was 24.

I remember getting a call from my immediate supervisor after I completed all the paperwork, shocked that I was so young; they assumed I was in my late 30s. I never intended to fool people; it just worked out that way. Since I had to grow up so fast and was essentially parenting myself, my parents, and siblings most of my life, I appeared very mature.

What's interesting is how wrong appearances can be. On one hand, I was incredibly mature for my age. My persona at this point, from years of being on my own, was Type A: hard-charging, competitive, assertive, disciplined, and an achiever.

I truly felt that this was who I was, and it wasn't until decades later, when I peeled back the layers of my ego and looked closely at the defense mechanisms in place, that I discovered otherwise.

I always seemed to walk into crazy, positive positions. In this new role, I had to secure space, arrange for renovations, hire staff, manage the staff, create business opportunities to earn a salary, and earn commissions on both my own sales and the office's sales. For the first year, the company paid me to oversee the building process, which amounted to an hour or two a week; the rest of the time, I renovated my rental properties.

By the second year, I was making $80,000 at 25 years old. By the time I was 27, I had saved $100,000. None of this fazed me, and it should have been a sign that my connection to my life was rather shaky. I completely missed it. I was on autopilot, doing what I thought I should do, what appeared to be what everyone else was doing. With virtually no guidance on true purpose and passion, I just kept working, saving, and bailing my family out.

* * *

When one defines their sense of self by the opinions of others, the door to manipulation by others becomes wide open.

The more successful I became, the more my family expected of me, and the more I felt obligated to them. I was always grateful for the money I was making and the safety net I had created as a result, and found it really hard not to help my family out. Somewhere along the line, I developed a very overblown sense of responsibility for keeping my family together, and the carrot was the expectation that I would help financially.

By now, Mother was even more jealous of me and took every opportunity to bring me down, always cleverly manipulating my emotions to get what she wanted and what she felt she deserved.

Even though I was living thirty miles away, her energy still affected me profoundly. She would call me completely drunk and trash the world, including me, and essentially make me feel terrible for her state compared to mine. More often than not, I would end up sending her money out of guilt.

Mother started working after her divorce and was completely resentful that she had to do what she deemed menial work. Her sense of entitlement was enormous, and it further solidified my sense of selflessness. Everything she was, I strived to be the opposite. I dreaded every phone conversation and finally refused to speak with her after 5 p.m., as she still adhered to the 5 p.m. drinking rule.

I found Mother's lack of gratitude appalling. My grandparents bailed my parents out financially for my entire childhood, and they continued to do so for Mother after their divorce. Mother was a prolific liar and manipulator, and as the oldest of her siblings by nine years and as a child spoiled rotten, she continued this pattern until my grandparents died. Sadly, one of the last things my grandmother said to me before passing was to "stop giving your mother money; she's just using you."

The only time Mother showed any positive emotion was when, one time in my frustration, I called Mother out on her self-centered, bitter, manipulative, entitled behavior and said I felt it came from her childhood. Mother said her parents were amazing, which struck me as an unbelievable acknowledgement, given that she was literally the worst in contrast. Clearly, her denial and delusion ran deep.

Because I always had an ample savings account, no boundaries, and was a severe codependent, Mother could use this to her advantage. What I find ironic is that she created my emotional deficiencies and then took advantage of me because of them. Mother never once saw anything wrong with taking money from me, and I always felt so sorry for her.

I saw nothing wrong with giving it to her, although she wasn't actually poor. I had this belief instilled in me from a very young age that I was more resilient, more capable, and more motivated—I actually believed God had given me these incredible gifts, and I developed these traits as a result—and I felt like everyone else wasn't playing on the same field.

Looking back, this was ridiculous on my part and part of the false self I lived with for a good part of my life. It seemed so natural. I never challenged my persona, and I was very successful; I was exactly what the world saw as "having one's act together."

Since then, I've come to realize that, on a "Soul level," we are all resilient and have exactly what we need; however, we need to get out of our ego to find it. Where I failed with myself, I had a PhD in fixing and helping others.

Chapter 2

*While my ego focused on "fixing" others,
my light was slowly being covered.*

✺

THE PART THAT no one questioned, myself included, was whether I was happy. I never overtly asked myself this question until the last several years. I didn't even realize I should ask this question.

Was I happy during this period?

I think if someone had asked me back then, I would have answered that I was, but that was because I had somehow escaped a childhood with no addictions or antisocial behavior that could have easily occurred under the circumstances.

Where I was at the moment was a significantly happier place. I never questioned whether this filled my Soul or whether my life purpose was being met; I was doing what I believed I was supposed to be doing.

Today, I can clearly see that I was so unhappy. I was born a free-spirited, sensitive, creative, gentle, and change-the-world-for-the-better type of person, and I had morphed into a Type A, high-charging, take-no-prisoners kind of person.

What's interesting to me is even though my career mirrored who I had become, my Soul always seemed to find a way to "poke" through. Even as early as 25, I had heard that funding was being cut at the children's services agency, so I organized a city-wide tag sale in the park, getting local businesses to donate their old inventory—we got new products to sell, they got the write-off.

When I look back, it's amazing to me that I couldn't see it. I was so conditioned to do what was practical that I was incapable of seeing what I needed. Early on, I learned to be selfless and that I couldn't be selfish in any manner. I didn't want people to view me as self-centered or entitled, so I made sure never to act that way.

Giving became my way of life. The more financially solid I became, the more gratitude I had, and the more I reached out to others. On a Soul level, I am truly service-driven, but I couldn't see the need for boundaries or the knowledge that I can't save everyone and that it's not my job to do so. The lens through which I viewed the world made me ripe to be manipulated for money.

Besides saving my family from themselves, I was extremely generous to friends, too generous in retrospect. From a young age, I always gave unconditionally, so they often manipulated me. I picked the wrong friends who I allowed to take advantage of me, and then, because I was so invested in the person, I would never let go of the relationship.

This pattern continued until recently; on some unconscious level, I tied my worth to what I did for others, and many people, unfortunately, many unsafe people, capitalized on this.

Letting go of people who don't serve my highest and best good has been a hard lesson for me. We each have these lessons. The nuances will be different, but these are the things required to understand and heal for our own emotional growth and well-being. Back then, I had no clue about any of this.

※ ※ ※

*When you're not living your passion,
boredom is just one knock away.*

After the mortgage company position, I got bored again. Still not seeing the pattern, I tried out real estate, which I did for a while. Then I was an appraiser, and then I was asked to start another mortgage company within a small bank. This appealed to me because I felt like I was a part of something more meaningful.

I again excelled, working around the clock, by introducing low-income mortgage financing to a small town where the bank had branches. I also created a land lease opportunity, which was touted as being way ahead of its time. I did all this with little fanfare. After having no accolades growing up, I internalized everything, and I never rested on my laurels. I would do something amazing and then move on to something else amazing. Clearly, I was looking for something. The problem was, I was looking in all the wrong places.

When I started at the bank, we were in the height of a commercial real estate boom, and the commercial lenders at the bank were granting commercial loans to virtually anyone who asked or had a heartbeat. Before long, our balance sheet was precarious, and then one Friday afternoon, unannounced, the feds came in and literally shut us down.

By Saturday at 9:00 a.m., we were a new bank with a new name, and everyone had to be interviewed for their role in the bank's demise. As an officer, I was at financial risk because many of my colleagues became financially liable and had to pay for their role in the poor lending policies. Fortunately, the SEC did not implicate me, and in fact, they gave me a huge raise to stay. As usual, none of this phased me, so I interviewed to see what other opportunities were available. I landed another role with a bigger company, which ultimately led me to my future husband.

Often, the Universe gives us a push, and we don't recognize it, but we feel compelled to move in another direction, even if it doesn't entirely make sense. I strongly believe this was the catalyst that pushed me, and as you will see, it sent me on a trajectory that has led me to where I am today and completely changed my life course. When you feel a push, it's so important to listen and, more importantly, to have faith in the direction you're going, even if it doesn't follow the course everyone else might take. It is important to listen and then get out of the way!

I started in this position, and like all the others, I made money, did my job well, got raises and advancements, but I knew I wouldn't be planting roots. Until the last minute, I was always willing to give my all. Out of the blue, again, I landed a position that became available at a bank owned by a brokerage firm. This firm was unknown to me, and the position was something I had never considered, but it intrigued me. I interviewed, and it turned out to be a brand new role, which appealed to me.

When they offered me the position, they gave me a salary package that was so generous I had to run it by others to see if I was missing something. Turns out I wasn't. The Universe will conspire to move us in the direction we need to be going, even if we are not aware that we are being nudged on a different path.

Within two weeks, I was working for the new company, and within a couple of months, I was making more money than I had ever dreamed of. I was an internal wholesaler, offering lending products to the financial advisors who sold the products to their clients.

What was baffling is that one product was a line of credit on a house, and the financial advisor and I would get paid even if the clients never used the line of credit. It was the worst management decision ever for the bank, but the best for the advisors, clients, and me.

I would sell the line of credit as an insurance policy in the event the client needed access to quick, short-term money without having to liquidate their stock portfolio. It was a fantastic sales pitch, a legitimate part of financial planning, and a super easy sell. This was so easy. The brokers were ecstatic, and I was making a killing. Again, the money never interested me. It was more about winning and success in building the network. I became very well-known and well-liked at the firm.

My personal life was okay, though not great. I had friends, but I never felt truly connected to anyone, mostly because my persona and ego were choosing my friends, not my Soul. Slowly, I was growing internally, but there was always a conflict between my career, which encompassed most of my life, and who I was trying to become. I was managing well, mainly focused on my career, and was getting over the first man who broke my heart.

My family continued to haunt me. Mother was so incredibly deficient. I learned that my great-grandmother had died months earlier, and I was never told. In fact, my mother mentioned it by saying, "When my grandmother died several months ago," failing to recognize her death affected me too.

Mother apparently forgot that her kids had also lost a relative. I said nothing because I knew what a waste of time any conversation with her was, still continuing to bail her out financially and offering emotional support as any "good parent" would, since that's how she subconsciously viewed my role.

During this period, my mother was dating and living with someone whom she was supposedly in love with. She called me one Saturday morning, and she sounded like death. I asked what was going on, and based on her response, I told her to hang up and call the squad immediately.

My instinct was spot on. I raced to the hospital 30 miles away and was told she should have died and had severe hepatitis. My mother played dumb and acted like she had no clue what had happened, and, when questioned, told me she knew nothing. I remember saying she needed to find out what had happened, and she told me to call her doctor.

It turns out Mother was playing one of her many games, because when I called the doctor, he was rude and annoyed with me for asking why he hadn't communicated with Mother. Turns out he had, and Mother, in reality, had poisoned herself with Tylenol and alcohol, a deadly combination, and was lucky to be alive.

I found out later that her live-in was moving, and even though he gave her the option of moving with him, she was used to getting her way, and she was trying to manipulate him into staying with her by deliberately overdosing. Apparently, her manipulations never changed; it didn't work, and he left her anyway. I was livid, realizing Mother was manipulating me again, and vowed to create some distance, though that was short-lived as always.

❋ ❋ ❋

The story we came to believe as a child creates the lens through which we see the world as adults.

Stepfather, by now, had taken an even more insignificant role in my external life and a much bigger role in my internal life than I ever realized. He was a full-fledged alcoholic as well, but didn't have the support of a family like Mother. At some point, I learned he was homeless and that someone took him in. When I caught up with him, he was living in a boarding house.

I still had not looked realistically at what he had done to me or his role in our family life, choosing to buy into the story that he was a good man because he provided for us, and, just as important, this is how a good girl acts. As always, I felt sorry for him, so during that period, I went on a spending spree and bought a winter wardrobe for him.

On this day, I went to my grandparents for the holidays. My mother was living with them at this point. She was drunk and boasting that Stepfather was homeless. This sickened and disgusted me, never mind that she was hurting my younger brothers. I dropped the wardrobe off to Stepfather, which was heartbreaking, went home, and told Mother never to mention Stepfather in that manner or I would never speak to her again. The risk of losing her "bank" was too much, so she never did.

Both parents continued to stress me out, triggering deep wounds from childhood and propelling me to work even harder. My life became a paradox. I was working with the biggest names in town, giving the illusion that I must have come from a wonderful family. I kept the vault safely locked because I knew the shameful truth, and the risk of being found out was too great.

I never mentioned to anyone on the planet how messed up my family life was. The shame and hurt were constant, but I stuffed them down. I really thought I was managing it all fairly well, and technically I was, but at an enormous cost to my True Self.

My career continued to zoom ahead. Money was pouring in, and I was saving like crazy, though never for material gain—it simply offered a sense of safety I couldn't yet find within myself. While I couldn't say I was happy, I was relatively content and definitely grateful for all that I had. I continued looking for charitable outlets, even becoming a trained facilitator for alcohol recovery groups. This seemed like a great way to give and to heal. However, it was short-lived because I couldn't stand the whining, entitlement, and lack of gratitude (an unfair assessment); it was everything I wanted to get away from.

I still ran most days, and I started delving deeper into personality theory and psychology, specifically Carl Jung. These interests and passions continue to this day. Again, my Soul was trying to sprout through the many layers of dirt (ego) I had thrown upon it, and I still wasn't making the connection.

Chapter 3

When someone shows you who they are, believe them.

—Maya Angelou

✺

IN THE SPRING of 1994, I received a call from a coworker who asked if I would consider a blind date for a business function. Never one to pass up an opportunity to further my career, I jumped at this opportunity. I remember the date was going to call me on a particular day to solidify plans, and when he didn't and the day was almost over, I called him instead.

Since he appeared shy, and I was less than enthusiastic about spending too much time with him, I agreed to meet him at the event. I was super excited about going to this business function, but not at all excited about my date—I was just making the best of it.

The night went smoothly, and when asked to all go to the buffet, there were two buffet tables. Everyone went to the same one except my date, Chuck, and me, who, independently of one another, went to the other. We both laughed at the lunacy of what we deemed the "sheep," and it was at this moment that I realized maybe he wasn't so bad.

Later that evening, the person who set up the blind date asked me what I thought, and I vividly remember saying, "It's not like we'll get married or anything, but we'll at least be friends." By the end of that year, we were married.

From that first date, we started hanging out, playing tennis, running together, cooking together, hosting dinners, and traveling. We kind of fell right into step. What I loved about Chuck initially became my biggest downfall. He asked very little about my family dynamics, and I was grateful that it didn't matter to him.

Chuck presented as a "good boy," played by the rules, and was well-mannered, smart, ambitious, and what I felt was a wonderful complement to me. We had so much fun together the first year, and I felt like I could be more myself with him, free-spirited for sure.

Were there red flags? Absolutely, but we felt so in sync we overlooked them. I vaguely explained my childhood and the fact that my parents were alcoholics, and that simple explanation seemed to satisfy him; he never asked more, so I never told more.

It never occurred to me that he might have had his own secrets, because of the story he told—perfect childhood, perfect college, maybe a bit shy with girls, but nothing concerning. I bought his story, and he bought mine. I was super happy to be moving towards being part of a healthy family.

I saw early on that Chuck was a conflict-avoidant and a pleaser, but I was a pleaser, too, so it didn't bother me. During the first year, there were a few instances where he would throw me under the bus, but I was so in love and had really no one to validate my feelings, so I ignored them all. This scenario played out over and over in my marriage.

The story that I will never forget happened a few months after I met Chuck. By now, people saw us as a couple, and we had already discussed marriage. Our values concerning kids, the future, and our long-term goals aligned—we seemed perfect for each other. Our company was a big sponsor of a local golf tournament, and I volunteered to help. We were on break, and we both had to use the restroom. Chuck was out in minutes, but the girl's line was a mile long.

I noticed some men were watching the men's bathroom door so their partner could use it without fear that someone would walk in. I suggested this to Chuck, and he agreed to watch the door while I used the bathroom, which was necessary because there was a long line of urinals and then one stall at the very end.

I did my business quickly, and suddenly, men started entering the bathroom. And then more men came in, and before long, I peeked out, and there were several men waiting in line to use the stall. I was essentially stuck and wondered what had happened to Chuck, but I was more intent on figuring out how to get out of the men's room.

Finally, with little choice, I announced that I was a girl, that I saw nothing, and asked if everyone could stop what they were doing so I could leave. I finally got out, and when I looked to find Chuck, he was calmly sitting at the bar having a beer. It turns out he left me when men showed up because it made it "uncomfortable" for him.

It shocked me, yet somehow I convinced myself it was no big deal. It was a bigger deal than I could have ever imagined. This became a huge theme in our marriage. Chuck never had my back, and I essentially recreated my childhood. It took me years to realize this since I was mostly living from my unconscious wounds, and even more years to realize the upset disguised the hurt, an emotion I had disowned in childhood.

There were other themes during that first year where I was always the bad cop, even if the problem wasn't mine. I was so accustomed to being on my own and having to do my own dirty work that I took it all on. Chuck loved being the good guy and had no problem with me being the "bad guy."

My sense of self was so weak that it was easy to have my boundaries violated. Plus, my codependency worked well in this relationship.

❋ ❋ ❋

When dysfunction and chaos are "familiar," it's really easy to overlook "red flags." In fact, often they don't seem like "red flags" at all until years later.

The summer of this same year yielded another red flag; I saw it, never forgot it, but didn't act on it, and it came back to haunt me. Over the weekend, Chuck was playing in a softball game, and while messing around, he re-injured his leg, which already had a torn ACL from a skiing accident.

On this day, he was seeing a surgeon to see what his options were. There were only two options, so it shouldn't have been too shocking either way. I came home after he did and found him sitting in the dark on the screened porch, drinking a beer, talking to his parents, and whining about how unfair life was, as if he were a little boy.

He didn't see me at first, but as soon as he did, his demeanor changed, and he quickly hung up. I remembered being completely unnerved by this since, up to that point, he had acted like he was emotionally self-sufficient, yet he had just shown me a very childish, immature side I couldn't reconcile. Instead, I pushed it aside, just as I had learned as a child.

Another red flag that would haunt me was his family dynamic, but I missed all of this. It's funny what registers in our head and heart, yet what we overlook when it doesn't fit the "relationship movie" we've created.

Chuck eventually had surgery, and his family came to help him, which I found extremely odd since he was 35 and had a girlfriend willing to help. Now, in fairness, my family would have never done this, so I always factored in that my lens might be inaccurate. Chuck blamed it on his parents wanting to be there. I'm not so sure.

Since I found the whole situation very awkward, I decided I would stay with him until 9 p.m. and sleep at my home. Chuck was having none of this and was adamant that I stay with him. I wasn't a fan of this idea, but weak boundaries ruled, so I stayed. The entire dynamic was strange, yet I allowed myself to ignore it.

The second notable thing was Chuck's interaction with his mother, which seemed very juvenile. We were playing cards one night, and Chuck had too much to drink and started singing some Pink Floyd song, accent and all, over and over. He was obnoxious and childish, yet his mother encouraged it and ate it up. I found it to be very uncomfortable, but again, I chalked it up to not having a normal parental relationship gauge.

There were smaller signs as well, like the time I went out with a girlfriend and got home later than I expected (this was long before cell phones), and he went ballistic, leaving the house for hours. Another instance was when I was going to the outlets with my girlfriends, and he insisted on going. Both of these pointed to his inability to be alone, which worked oddly well with the anxious attachment I had adopted; none of this was conscious.

* * *

Slowly but surely, we fell into our childhood dynamics. The problem is, neither of us felt it happening, and it was anything but healthy.

Officially, we were to get married in December 1994, but it was totally stressing me out. The guest list had grown to over three hundred by now. We were paying for it all, and it was becoming more of an event than a wedding. I had a lot of reservations about having a wedding this size and, besides the cost, was afraid my family would cause a scene.

I divulged none of my worries to Chuck. For all I knew, he had his own, but when I suggested eloping during the Christmas holiday while in Ohio with his family, he was on board. Everything about this was wrong. My lack of emotional availability, his lack of interest in my inner life, the idea of getting married half-baked, all wrong, but I was relieved.

I literally called every state neighboring Ohio to see who could quickly marry us, eventually settling on Kentucky since there wasn't a waiting period. This became another theme: I took care of everything, and Chuck went along for the ride.

We drove to Kentucky on December 27 and were married that day. No fanfare, no powerful emotions, just two emotionally unavailable, successful adults who did not know what we were in store for. I believe we loved each other, but we were so emotionally ill-equipped that it wasn't at all what it should have been.

Essentially, we were two unconscious people finding one another, hoping the other could provide the sense of safety and love we couldn't provide ourselves. In Love relationships, we attract at the level of woundedness or the level of wisdom; we chose the former.

Within a few months after we got married, we decided we would move back to Chuck's hometown. Chuck was now managing a brokerage office and had his own retail clients, many of whom were from his hometown. And for the long-term plan of starting a family, this made sense.

Plus, in my opinion, any plan to distance myself from my family was a good plan. Before long, we had convinced our company to let us move, and they were happy to have my willingness to establish the bank's presence in Ohio.

We had a few obstacles to overcome. We both had houses that were seriously underwater, and Connecticut was in a housing recession. However, not to be deterred, we rented out our homes and moved to Ohio. The plan was to move in with Chuck's parents for ten days until our temporary apartment was available.

I felt I was moving much closer to happiness and was genuinely thrilled to be a part of Chuck's family, as he described it to me. Little did I know my dream family would turn into a nightmare.

❋ ❋ ❋

When the story you were taught as a child turns out to be a lie, how do you trust?

Almost as soon as we moved into Chuck's parents' house, it all seemed wrong. Early in the first week of our arrival, we lost a baby. Truthfully, I didn't know how to react emotionally. The O.J. trial was ongoing at the time, and when I tried to call Chuck to tell him, he put me on hold so he could hear the verdict.

In the meantime, I went back to his parents, and although they tried to be kind, they were just emotionally detached. Chuck's sister had a rec volleyball game that evening and was short players, so rather than have Chuck stay with me, which would have been kind and natural under the circumstances, his mother was insistent that he play volleyball so they didn't forfeit. This was shocking, but with little support, I let it go.

The next night, I had promised Mother I would call her, which was always a stressful ordeal. I felt very guilty for having left her, and I knew I was going to hear about it. By now, Chuck should have been, or was, aware of this dynamic.

As I was waiting to call, Chuck's sister invited him to a bar, and he went. It left me with his parents to fend for myself, and he showed up hours later, completely drunk. This wasn't the first time I saw him drunk, but it was the first time I sensed there might be more to his drinking than I realized.

The dynamic between Chuck's mother and Chuck escalated, and every night after work, he would fall into a chair, seeking her sympathy for what a hard day he had, even though my day was even harder since I was starting over.

Chuck's sister practically lived with the family, though she owned a condo, and both she and Chuck always had a beer in their hands after a certain hour. Within a day or two, it became clear which roles each of them occupied in their family.

Chuck carried the image of an independent, successful, hardworking superstar; his sister was the opposite. In both cases, each was striving in their own way to get their emotional needs met, albeit dysfunctionally.

Both were being emotionally enabled by my mother-in-law, who had her own issues, so allowing her adult children to depend on her felt good. Not too dissimilar from my behavior. Either way, this was not the family I signed up for, and I remember calling a girlfriend back in CT, telling her if I hadn't left my job and rented my home, I would have left immediately. It was unfortunate because it never got better.

Finally, our apartment was ready, and we moved out. At least I had a little relief from the craziness, but I was definitely unnerved and didn't know what to make of it. Part of the problem is that I didn't clearly understand what a "normal family" was, but I was pretty sure this family wasn't it. Chuck and I were both very ambitious, and work, though stressful, fell into place. We worked, worked out, and really, we were quite content.

I was very leery of my in-laws and started keeping my distance and lowering my expectations. Chuck's role in the family was that of the golden child and successful kid, and in this way, we aligned. Consciously, we were both achievers who paid for our own schooling and never expected or asked for a dime from our families. The major difference was that Chuck's mother put him on a pedestal, while mine was jealous and did everything possible to knock me down. Whereas I developed the ability to self-regulate, he needed reassurance, and it was these subconscious needs that actually attracted us; we just weren't conscious enough to understand the marriage contract we entered.

As time wore on, I would take on the role of mother, he the child. In perfect alignment, connected by our complementary, yet dysfunctional, subconscious programming.

Chapter 4

My marriage became stable. The problem is, it was dysfunctionally stable.

✸

AROUND THIS TIME, we decided it was time to have a baby, and I got pregnant the first month. Nervous would best describe how I felt about becoming a parent.

Unlike many of my peers, I didn't have any positive parenting role models, so I was fully aware of both the responsibility and the gravity of raising a child. I was deeply afraid of not being enough. I read every book on the subject, hoping to learn the skills that others were taught by their own parents.

This is when I first began noticing more serious cracks in my marriage. My husband was as clueless as I was about positive parenting, and yet he still hung onto the idea that his childhood was perfect. It wasn't long before the cracks became fractures.

Prior to getting pregnant, our social life centered on activities, many of which involved drinking. To me, this was just a part of the activity and nothing more. Having grown up with alcoholics, I was very aware of the possible genetic connections and monitored my drinking compulsively. I never drank to avoid or escape, and, unfortunately, I made the mistake that Chuck was coming from the same perspective.

I didn't drink during my pregnancy, but it didn't stop my husband. The problem became even more highlighted since I wasn't drinking. I knew he was drinking too much too often, and I started seeing a pattern that I had missed previously. Chuck would grab a beer as soon as he walked in the door, and it would continue until bedtime. I also started noticing that he never seemed to get inebriated, which I knew was not a good sign.

If things went badly at work, the drinking became greater. If things went great, it was time to celebrate. Basically, like my parents, there was never a reason not to drink. Around this time, I expressed my concerns and resentment that he checked out most of the nights, and he would either reassure me I was overreacting because of my childhood or get angry, and I would drop it.

As my pregnancy progressed, I sensed an uptick in his drinking, and this became a greater issue. It became a constant cycle of my complaining, his denial, my making threats, and his promising to curb his drinking. Rinse, repeat.

One night, around the sixth month of my pregnancy, we went out with friends. I was less than thrilled since I knew it would be an invitation for my husband to drink and, to the best of my knowledge, he had cut back. The last thing he needed was an excuse to drink more. The night started fine, but went downhill pretty fast. My husband was drinking ridiculous amounts—I did not know at this point that he suffered from social anxiety since he hid it—and I finally told him it was time to leave. He refused.

I ended up going home myself, and he got a ride, waking me up at 2 a.m., vomiting everywhere, and confusing the closet for the bathroom. This was an exact replication of my childhood, and I was sick to my stomach. Here I was: a new city, a new career, a home in CT rented, no local friends, and pregnant. I was right back where I had started 35 years earlier.

I have never felt so unarmed in my life.

Being pregnant limited my options, and I really felt trapped. As a last resort, I reached out to his parents for help and support and was told that "I was pushing Chuck too hard, and that's why he drinks so much."

Yeah, not exactly what I expected, though in retrospect I should have known better. I had thought I had picked a man who had his act together, who could take the reins once in a while, and instead, I found a man who was just great at hiding his lack of maturity. Worse was that his parents couldn't see it and blamed me.

I finally gave Chuck an ultimatum and forced him into couples therapy, which lasted one session since the therapist essentially told Chuck he had a drinking problem and needed to grow up. Chuck's compromise was that he would stop drinking so much, and my compromise was that I believed him.

Both were ridiculous.

Chuck's drinking was a constant theme in our marriage, but I wasn't blameless. I was so intent on creating the stable family that I never had. I took everything on myself. The environment I grew up in created an extraordinarily resilient person, and my codependency caused me to shield my emotionally weaker husband from all things that challenged his emotional stability.

I didn't do this overtly. I just recreated both of our childhood dynamics, which is all we knew. It seemed to work because, as far as I could tell, he didn't drink as much. I later found out he just didn't drink as much in front of me, and I was in total denial about how big the problem was going to become.

As I focused on getting ready for our son, life kind of fell into a rhythm. The thing that my husband did for me was allow me to financially and emotionally support my family. I used to think this was an act of kindness, but I have now come to realize I do not know what he thought. I'm leaning more towards the idea that as long as his needs were being met, everything else had nothing to do with him.

Boundaries were weak with everyone, and I did not know. I kept every figurative ball in the air, made every decision for the family, and did virtually all the household management, bill paying, taxes, and vacation planning—all while making as much money and working as hard as my husband.

I had done this for so long that it just felt normal. Before long, there wasn't one thing I wasn't doing in our home and life. His only task was mowing the lawn and taking out the garbage. Everything else was my responsibility. Still, it worked because we were dysfunctionally in balance, and despite my exhaustion in trying to keep it all together, there was a sense of safety in the control. I was nervous about my ability to raise my son in the best way possible, although I was proficient at raising others, including myself, my parents, brothers, friends, and now my husband.

We were still working at the office together before my son was born, and we were asked to take a personality test for management training. I was already deep into Carl Jung and Myers-Briggs personality testing, so this was enjoyable and intriguing since, by then, I was already "typing" people as a matter of routine.

I knew I was an ENFP and that my husband was an ISTJ—opposites in personality, but a great romantic match, assuming one's maturity showed up. I started telling my peers before they got their test scores back what I guessed they were. In all 23 cases, except for my husband, I was correct.

My husband tested as an ESFJ, which was confusing. An ESFJ is gregarious, a people lover, outgoing, friendly, a superb organizer, and wears their emotions on their sleeves, deeply caring about others. Conversely, my husband was introverted, emotionally distant, bothered by people's emotions, quiet, and so on.

This made me realize he did not know who he was. It rattled me so much that I challenged him, and he couldn't answer why he responded like he did—huge red flag. Years later, when he was relatively sober, he took another test and tested as an ISTJ. Turns out, I wasn't the only one who was clueless.

The two best traits I learned from childhood were gratitude and not dwelling on the past. Tomorrow will always be better. I still have these qualities today, but with much less idealism. Back then, I would uncover something really troubling, attempt to fix it, and then move past it, regardless of the magnitude or red flags.

My husband always presented as a man of the highest integrity and a 'good boy', so when he told me something, I believed him. His goodness fed into my feelings of badness about myself. A prominent trait of alcoholism (most addictions) is lying, and this trait didn't miss my husband, yet I was oblivious to it.

Looking back, this is another one of my flaws. I had to accept so much contradictory behavior in my parents; I grew accustomed to downplaying the bad in favor of the good. Toxic behavior not only felt normal, but it also felt like home.

When I was a child, this was a matter of survival. As an adult, it was dysfunctional; I did not know how detrimental this was. The longer this went on, the more emotions got buried, the more emotionally independent I became, and the more emotionally detached my husband became—we had both recreated familiarity and the dynamic of our family of origin. The problem is, neither of us knew the cost.

So, as my pregnancy progressed, we got into a rhythm. I can't say that Chuck wasn't attentive or disregarded my pregnancy, although, looking back, he was mostly detached. I knew this then but assumed it was more a product of my carrying our son and being already emotionally bonded, something he couldn't appreciate.

It bothered me that he refused to read a parenting book, and if I mentioned this, he might pick it up for a page or two. I was becoming more and more self-contained and scared to death about my ability to raise a child. My fears were ever-present, though never expressed to Chuck, and I realized I had moved him off the square from having the ability to support me emotionally to being a "doer" if I asked him.

I think Chuck knew he was lacking, and he made up for it by running errands or going grocery shopping with me. Although I think the fact that he expressed his dislike for being alone a few years into the marriage was a greater motivator than the desire to share the experience. On some level, I knew this was all wrong and not a healthy, mature relationship, but I buried that thought.

From Chuck's perspective, he liked the arrangement. He had all the trappings of a solid family, but with little emotional or energetic investment. From my end, my emotional needs became nonexistent. Little did I know I became Chuck's mother, in charge of everything and the decision maker, while he became my stepfather and mother and acted more like another child in the family, and was emotionally uninvested.

Chapter 5

When you become programmed to believe you have no needs, you ask for no needs to be met, and that is exactly what you will get.

✹

WHILE THERE WERE moments of tension during my pregnancy, everything went rather smoothly until week twenty, when I had an AFP test and the results were not good. Because of my age, I had a high-risk doctor, and he spared no effort.

When he called me with the AFP test results, I was at work, and he told me that the test results should have been in the 450 range, while mine were below 100. This meant there was a very significant possibility of a baby with Down syndrome, and I would need an amniocentesis to get a clear determination. I remember sitting at my desk, shocked, but also removed from the gravity of the situation. My childhood prepared me well for difficult emotional situations. It also primed me well for my husband's reaction, which was nonexistent. I needed something from him, but truthfully didn't even know what it was. I just knew I felt unprepared for this, though in some ways it didn't surprise me since I was very used to life's curveballs.

So we had the amniocentesis, which carried a risk of miscarriage, and awaited the results, which were negative. What's interesting is that, looking back, Chuck and I didn't discuss the emotional impact this was having. I believe he just didn't get it, and I isolated, which he didn't get either.

We were moving further and further apart just when we needed to be moving closer and closer together. There was a significant lack of emotional reciprocity on my husband's part, which I failed to notice. I continued supporting him, as any good parent would, since this is how the relationship progressed. He accepted my emotional support and nurturing as if it were his due, with no effort required; it was all he knew, and also all I knew.

Basically, the blind leading the blind.

It was around this time that I remember an exchange my husband and mother-in-law had that made me realize I was up against a bigger dynamic than just Chuck and me. We were at Chuck's parents' house, and his mother was telling a story, which, in itself, was unusual. She typically let everyone else dominate the conversation.

In the middle of the conversation, Chuck cut her off, switching to a different topic. I was so dumbfounded that she didn't react that I spoke up on her behalf. Instead of gratitude, she told me, "I don't mind," and she let Chuck continue the story. I sat there incredulously, and later, I tried discussing the situation with Chuck. He saw nothing wrong with his behavior because, to him, "Mom didn't mind."

Another huge red flag.

There's an old philosophy that says how men treat their moms is how a significant other can expect to be treated. This theory was correct in my marriage.

Finally, nine months had passed, and the nursery was ready; I was ready. My company let me work from home—long before it was common—so I assumed I would work, nurse, take care of my son, and all would be good. I was wrong.

First, I was two weeks overdue and never dilated, so we calmly left work to pack at home and then drove to the hospital. By now, I was an expert at dissociating, and everything seemed to happen outside of me. It was very surreal. The doctor induced me, and after 36 hours of hard labor, I was told I was finally getting both an epidural (finally!) and a C-section.

It devastated me. Surgery did not fit into my master plan and the need to be in control. It was chaotic and stressful, but my son was born less than ten minutes after they decided. I was crying the entire procedure, and my husband was literally blank and watching from afar, allowing others to comfort me.

In his defense, I am sure he felt shocked as well, but his inability to even attempt to comfort me would have been shocking to anyone else in this situation. The hospital stay went from two days to five, and I was so overwhelmed that I was in no hurry to leave.

Plus, for the first time in my life, I was actually being cared for. I had a small insight that this is probably how Mother felt during all her hospital stays. A great insight, yet I was still too entrenched in my childhood story to allow myself to see Mother from a different lens.

Chuck worked during the week, so I rarely saw him; I was always worried about his need to work, taking on his stress from his need to work, and I didn't want to stress him further. On Friday, when he could have spent the night, he had a club function he had promised to sell tickets for and left me alone at the hospital.

What's so amazing is that I thought it was normal. I expected nothing from him emotionally, which is how I would treat my children. He ended up coming back around 10 p.m. when someone blatantly called him out for not being with his wife and newborn.

I asked for nothing because that was what Chuck could give and what I knew, and my only support system, his family, thought it was normal as well. Add to the mix that I grew up knowing I was on my own. I had literally recreated the emotional dynamic of my childhood, as did he.

✻ ✻ ✻

Life wasn't perfect. In fact, there was always a sense that something "big" was missing, but compared to childhood, it was a utopia.

Despite everything, I was as happy as I had ever been. I had a beautiful baby boy, and while Chuck and I did not become more emotionally connected, we still shared very similar values and built a life for ourselves. We were always fortunate to make a lot of money and to capitalize on the industry we were in.

Both of us were huge savers, and although we seemed to have a lot externally, we always lived well below our means. We were frugal and made wise financial decisions early on, and this is where we excelled as a couple. We also loved our son equally, and although I handled the day-to-day tasks, I believe my husband genuinely enjoyed our son and being a father.

The first few days after coming from the hospital, I felt like I had finally figured out this baffling world I had grown up in, and the magnitude of what I had gone through became even clearer.

I loved my son so much, and it was impossible for me to reconcile that my parents could have willingly and knowingly caused so much emotional pain and damage to their children. I knew before my son was even born that I would easily give up my life for him, and it was even stronger after.

What I knew was I loved my son more than I could ever believe, and with this, I had so much fear; I had never emotionally invested in anything so much, and I remember for many, many years feeling so afraid of something terrible happening to him. I knew this was irrational and leftover from childhood, but without a sounding board, it lingered much longer than it should have.

What surprises me now, looking back, is that I never thought to seek counseling at this point. I was so successful and fit everyone's definition of having my act together that I really didn't think I was as fear-driven or ego-driven as I turned out to be. The problem was that the fear was inside, buried deeply. It was moving me further and further away from my truth and Light, and I was completely unaware.

As the Universe would have it, my son came into this world ceremoniously, and he didn't skip a beat. He cried for the first three months, ten hours if it was a good day, fifteen if it was a difficult night. I breastfed until seven weeks, when we took him to his doctor to figure out what we were doing wrong, and we were told he was colicky and needed a special formula.

I was relieved there was a name for my son's malady and very dismayed to find the only cure was time. The nurses on this day commented that they hadn't heard a baby scream like he did in years. It was the guttural cry of a wounded animal. I remember telling my mother-in-law how stressful it was, and she dismissed me, saying, "All babies cry," which only made me feel inept and invalidated.

I will say my husband was great during this time. While he struggled to be emotionally available for me, he was wonderful at offering physical support in caring for our baby. Changing diapers, feedings, and getting up in the middle of the night were never a problem. Chuck was ideally suited to caring for a baby, as to the best of his ability, he really wanted to do what was right, which included being a responsible dad. A baby did not challenge his emotional unavailability.

His struggle intensified as Kevin grew older and life became increasingly emotionally complicated. We were told that there was no cure and that he would outgrow the colic by month three, and if it got terrible, we could put him in his crib and let him cry it out. It seemed like a brilliant plan, but I couldn't bring myself to do it. It was too close to the abandonment I felt as a child, and Chuck and I vowed to hold our son as long as we needed to so he always felt loved. We did this for three months straight, and I was beyond exhausted carrying the bulk of the responsibility.

By week eight, I was working out of the house and caring for a colicky newborn, and I was not managing well. Finally, by week ten, I realized something had to give, and I told Chuck I wanted to stop working. By now, we were both making the same and bringing in close to $500,000, but we were living as if we were making $100,000, so it was doable. His response was no way, no discussion, just "No!"

It turns out that, even though he touted how he wanted to support his family, he actually didn't want the responsibility. No matter how much I pleaded that I was missing out on the joy of having a baby, and the stress was too much, he wouldn't see it.

So, I gave in and continued working, although I decided I needed a nanny at home with me. I continued to take care of everything else: our son, the house, and our personal life. Boundary issues remained a huge theme in my marriage, but I never noticed. Everything felt familiar, and during this time, familiarity was not a bad thing; it allowed me to control everything and feel relatively safe.

We got into rhythm, and finally, my son stopped crying nonstop. I recall right around three months, as the doctor predicted, my son didn't cry for hours, and I was so totally freaked out, I called a nurse friend and asked what was wrong, should

I take him to the doctors, should I wake him up, and of course her response was, "No, this is what normal babies do."

I believed her, but I sat by my son's crib the entire night, afraid something was wrong. This feeling of doom never really left me. The colic didn't help, but what really hurt me was my childhood. I was so accustomed to preparing for things going wrong that I was constantly afraid something would happen to my son.

My depth of love for him was so strong, fear consumed me, and I was afraid I would miss something and that he would become ill or die at my own hands. I didn't realize how off this was until I explained it to someone else who had just had a newborn, and she said it wasn't her experience.

Owing to my childhood and not having the ability to control the outcome in every scenario, I felt very consumed by my irrational feelings, and this really affected my parenting. Not having good parenting modeled, I was trying to be the best parent with no storehouse of information and no adult to ask, both on my side and Chuck's.

Chuck's perspective was completely the opposite; he accepted this all casually since he always had his needs met, so he assumed I would take care of anything that was necessary. We were at polar ends of the spectrum, and I felt completely overwhelmed and under-supported.

I don't want to give the impression that everything was all bad because it wasn't. Compared to every other relationship, including both our families of origin, my marriage was great. This obscured most problems. When one's internal compass becomes distorted, we don't have the tools to recognize how off things are.

On the surface, and certainly looking from the outside in, we looked like we had it all. We were professionally successful, appeared to have a vibrant relationship, and dedicated ourselves to being the best parents we could be.

The problem is that the outside only showed a glimpse of us. During the first few years of my son's life, things were going well, even if we were drifting further apart emotionally. This we didn't see. My husband was excelling at his stock brokerage business and literally riding high. He was on top of the world, and this translated to him being more pleasant to be around and more attentive. What I was not yet aware of was what would happen when things weren't going great in the stock market.

Safety motivated me to protect our future, and the brokerage business played into this. By now, we had amassed a very sizable nest egg, and we set up our financial future for the rest of our lives if we took what we had saved up to this point and invested it moderately.

I thought Chuck and I agreed.

We had decided in 1999 to purchase a different home, as our businesses had grown significantly. We could then switch to another firm, which would offer us a signing bonus to bring our business to them. This bonus would be used to pay off our new home. I had agreed to join him in the brokerage business as a partner, and I began getting the requisite licenses.

This allowed me to negotiate our bonus, location, job title, etc., which I was much more effective at than Chuck, who had only worked at one company throughout his entire career. I never saw the problem with this, although, looking through my lens today, I see I was mothering my husband, even in the business arena.

We finally chose a company that seemed to be a good fit. They gave me a VP title and Chuck SVP; we moved our clients over, and I began the arduous process of getting all my brokerage licenses.

For a while, we were very proud of our accomplishments. We purchased our last home, which I'm still living in, and saved enough by our late thirties to know we would retire comfortably, even if we never saved another dime.

    We already had a sizable college fund for our then-three-year-old. Things were finally in a very calm place. I was relieved to find that my husband and I were seemingly in accord, at least financially. His drinking, not so much.

Chapter 6

*When you believe drinking is the problem instead
of a symptom, healing becomes impossible.*

✳

HAVING GROWN UP with the effects of drinking my whole life, I was becoming less and less tolerant of my son being exposed to Chuck's need for a few beers every day after work. I strongly felt it was sending a message that this is what adults do, even if he wasn't a confirmed problem drinker at this point. This became a constant theme in our home and one I wouldn't let up on.

By now, we were in a relatively comfortable routine, and I just couldn't fathom why he had to drink every night. I naively did not factor in that Chuck had different thoughts and needs on the subject, and it was a constant source of stress for me.

When we moved into the new home, which was larger and required more upkeep, I began something I called "the honor system." What this meant was that instead of dividing chores, we would both chip in when we could. If you honestly had the time to do a chore that needed to be done, then you would do it.

Chuck agreed with this philosophy, except as time went on, he didn't abide by it. Before long, I was doing even more—100 percent of the chores, dinner, social life, managing my son, planning vacations, paying bills, laundry, cleaning the house, planning and making meals, home maintenance—the two things my husband did were mow the lawn, which he liked, and invest our money, which was part of his day to day already.

My sense of over-responsibility and being a parent since childhood matched his learned helplessness and entitlement from his childhood. The problem is that it's insidious, and I was in a familiar, though dysfunctional, mode before I even realized what had happened. We continued in a dysfunctional equilibrium, stable but not healthy.

Every once in a while, I would have moments where I would acknowledge things were unfair, particularly when Chuck drank too much, and he couldn't even be healthily present for my son. His drinking started really affecting our marriage, and I began seeing things I didn't want to see.

One thing that stood out was that he seemed to drink more when he had a bad day or when he had a great day to celebrate, which was very similar to my childhood. The other thing that bothered me was that, although he loved our son fully, he seemed to derive his own emotional needs from our son instead of the other way around.

I started noticing this pattern when my son was three and should have been moving toward more independence. When he was younger, my son had always been very underweight, so a large focus was on making sure he ate enough. For the first two or three years, we spent a lot of time trying to get him to eat enough each day, which often involved feeding him while he was playing.

After a few years of this, we were told to "back off, and he'll eat when he's hungry." This, of course, brought up all kinds of childhood triggers for me, but I knew his doctor was right. So, Chuck and I agreed to back off, except Chuck didn't.

I chased my son to get him to eat more because I had this deep-seated irrational fear he would die. Chuck fed him to meet his own emotional needs. When I stopped essentially enabling my son's eating, my husband didn't, and the behavior became highlighted.

I started seeing a correlation between when I called him out on his drinking and how much he doted on our son. He felt abandoned by me, so he turned to my son to meet his emotional needs. This became another daily battle along with his drinking.

* * *

Never believe appearances unconditionally. What goes on behind closed doors could be much different.

The biggest issue, which allowed us to continue fooling ourselves, was that from the outside, we appeared to be the perfect family. No one had any clue that the division of labor and emotional support was completely one-sided, and I was so accustomed to juggling nonstop, our false life appeared seamless.

Couple that with my commitment to keeping family secrets safely in the vault, and we had the image of "perfect." The problem is that I was losing more and more of myself, the person I was just beginning to get to know. Prior to meeting Chuck, my true self became more present, and it wasn't Type A, but instead, free-spirited and easy-going. Within a few months of meeting Chuck, gone was the free-spirited girl who was just emerging, reverting to the Type A, controlling person who worked at full throttle 24/7 to keep life progressing.

I quickly got all my brokerage licenses and then negotiated with the bank that had purchased our brokerage firm for a bank position so I could cross-sell the brokerage business with my husband. This was all legit by bank policy, but my motivation was an underlying fear that my husband couldn't do it on his own.

Sadly, I never stopped helping him, even if it was to my detriment, because he had proven over and over that he was incapable of being the rock he let everyone think he was. In the early 2000s, we were at our peak in all aspects, and I thought we agreed financially. I trusted my husband in what he did and what he claimed to believe, until I realized that, financially, we had been on different pages the entire time.

He had invested heavily in tech stocks, as many had, and though he promised that when it reached a certain value, he would get out, he didn't. When the market crashed, we crashed right along with it. To say it shocked me is an understatement; however, I knew we could make it back, so I buckled down and sought other solutions.

Mother, though living close to 500 miles away, still wielded enormous power in my life. The "good daughter," without exception, and still the recipient of my mother's constant "feel sorry for me" calls, I would always send money and invite her on vacations.

My husband, now fully entrenched in the parent/child dynamic, questioned nothing. Mother continued to be treated like a queen when she was with us, and she never acknowledged appreciation at all.

Survivor's guilt was constant at this point.

I was financially stable and had an objectively good life. I was always bailing everyone out. My husband took this as part of what he had to allow to get me to do the things I did for him. My husband and Mother were not drastically different in how they used me, though I believe my husband loved me in his own way, not unlike Mother.

What always struck me as funny was that at one point, Mother was at my house, and she said to me, "You know Chuck takes advantage of you." I was speechless. I did not respond until years later, but she was right. By then, everyone was taking advantage of me, and I let them.

A few things happened around this time that I now see differently. Mother's car was in an accident in the parking lot where she worked, and the person didn't come forward. She called me crying that she didn't have money for the deductible, and, as always, I paid $500.

Years later, she was debating what to do with the car, and she let it slip that it had never been involved in an accident or had bodywork. I never found out what she used the money for. Similar things like this happened periodically, and I would always allow her to manipulate me.

She cried, usually drunk, about some crisis, and because my life was decent, I buckled and gave her what she needed. Guilt was always right under the surface. I never questioned the story or whether it was appropriate for Mother to ask for money. I was so conditioned to feeling guilty and giving; it was all I knew.

Even later, when my grandmother was dying and she told me to stop giving Mother, her daughter, money because she was purposely manipulating and using me, I couldn't break the pattern. The guilt was too much to bear. It was easier to give her money than feel bad.

✳ ✳ ✳

It's sad when chaos seems more "normal" than Peace.

When 9/11 hit, Mother's employer was being sold, and that was our next crisis. True to form, Mother called, crying about how she was going to lose her job—a job she claimed to hate—and mentioned it every chance she got. It wasn't that she hated the job as much as she thought she shouldn't have to work; her sense of entitlement was so strong.

Naturally, since solving everyone's problems was now a deeply ingrained part of my psyche, I started trying to find solutions. Every viable solution I offered, Mother found problems with. She drank, and I tried to fix. And then someone robbed her, and Mother really took on the victim role and went down the rabbit hole.

I felt bad about her being robbed, feeling it was a deep personal violation of space. Since I was really the parent in our relationship, it became a huge burden to shoulder, made bigger because I had a young child, was working full time, and was still trying to manage my marriage and my husband's drinking.

Mother's reaction to her problems was, until the day she died, "I'm the victim, and I should just kill myself." This, of course, brought up all kinds of psychological triggers in me. Mother used "killing herself" as her prime tool of manipulation and defense mechanism, and it worked exceptionally well.

From Ohio, I was now trying to find places for her to move and for alternative employment. Life was very hectic for me, with no emotional support from anyone, and I was trying to handle every ball in the air. Mother's place was not safe, and she needed to move sooner rather than later. And I was not getting help from anyone. I had to travel to CT frequently to explore housing options, consider job choices, and even deal with the insurance company regarding the stolen items. Essentially, I was a full-time parent, and Mother was a full-time child.

It became apparent that there would be a gap of time between apartments, and Mother would need a place to live. The obvious place to live was with my grandparents, but like a child, Mother refused to ask. So I had to make the call, which did not go well.

Apparently, after my parents' divorce, when Mother lived there for a year, it was a disaster. Mother was always drunk, belligerent, threatening suicide, smoking so much in her room that it had to be painted, obnoxious, negative, and never helped one bit. Basically, exactly how I remembered her.

I had to beg my grandparents to let her stay there for three months with ground rules. I can't express enough how pathetic it was to have to beg Mother's own parents and then admonish Mother on how to behave. Mother denied her previous behavior, which made things harder. I'm not sure what her emotional level was, but I know it was way below what it should have been.

David and I moved Mother to my grandparents over the weekend. Mother more or less watched and complained. Of course, I paid for the U-Haul, packing boxes, and other expenses; there were no other expectations. I was there to serve Mother.

Honestly, why I never walked away is quite hard to believe. I really felt completely brainwashed into thinking it was my job to take care of her. It never once occurred to me that my compulsion to take care of her was emotional abuse from Mother and an emotional distortion on my end. My grandparents were icy cold and not at all pleased. I couldn't wait to get out of there as quickly as possible. I don't blame my grandparents at all.

Chapter 7

Trying to help someone who really doesn't want to be helped is akin to pushing a rock up a mountain.

✺

OVER THE NEXT several weeks, I attempted to find Mother a new apartment while she continued complaining. Soon, I realized I would need to subsidize her rent for at least $350 per month, so I started thinking of other solutions. I started researching opportunities in Ohio, and it occurred to me that I could purchase a condo for a lower monthly outlay, and Mother would have better employment opportunities here.

Chuck was onboard, which was no surprise, and Mother, though she hated change, was up for anything that would benefit her. I quickly found a condo a few miles away, and within a month, I purchased it.

What stands out in my mind is how completely oblivious Mother was to the entire move and condo purchase. She sat back and let me do it all, occasionally complaining and playing the "woe is me" card to the fullest. The entire situation stressed me beyond belief, but you would never know it.

In those days, I didn't acknowledge negative emotions. I forged ahead and just made it happen, whatever needed to happen. Part of me knew my grandparents were failing, so this was also a way to take some burden off of them; I imagined they were relieved to get her out from under their responsibility.

The plan was for Mother to move and stay with us for the first two weeks until the condo was ready. I recall coming home on the first day and Mother seeing condos within half a mile of my house and saying that they would be perfect, completely unconcerned that they would cost five times more than hers.

What bothered me about this interaction was that I sensed she truly believed she was owed a condo because I had the resources. She was Mother, forgetting completely that since six and maybe earlier, she had only been my mother in name. Although the condo I had chosen for her was not as expensive, it was a brilliant solution for everyone. It was on the top floor, had a great private balcony, and was very affordable.

The two weeks my mother stayed with us while waiting for the condo to be ready were one of the two longest weeks of my life. I made it clear she was not to get drunk because I would not allow my son to be exposed to her in that manner, and she had to smoke outside for the same reason. The smoking she was fine with, the drinking she hid.

I had experienced her sense of entitlement and victimhood over the years, and up close, having spent weeks vacationing with her, staying at my house was a completely different story altogether.

First, I didn't trust her for many reasons, but mostly I didn't trust her with my son. Mother was jealous and vindictive, and I had an overwhelming sense that Mother was not above harming my child to get back at me. I was on pins and needles the entire two weeks and literally didn't sleep for fear she would do something terrible in the middle of the night to harm my son.

Nothing ever happened, and perhaps it was unfounded, but I had spent my entire life fully aware that Mother did everything she could to undermine me, all the while reaping the financial rewards for my hard work.

I now realize I kept trying to reach for the fantasy that if I tried harder, if I loved more, that I could have a happy family. I'm so sad as I write this, realizing I chased this carrot my entire life, and I would never catch it. In fact, my real growth was finally understanding this.

Things seemed to go fine for the first two days, and then we went out to a better-than-average dinner; that's when things hit the fan. I took Mother to this restaurant to make her feel good, have a substantial meal, and to celebrate her new life. My biggest mistake was that I had forgotten Mother had a need to either be above someone or feel inferior.

Because the restaurant was a bit more upscale, people dressed accordingly. I could tell she was acting very oddly and uncomfortably, which sadly ruined the meal. Mother never saw her issues as her issues. They had to be everyone else's, too, so dinner couldn't end soon enough.

When we got home, she went to her room, only to come out later, very drunk and ranting and raving. This was one of her biggest violations ever to me. Now she involved my son, and that was not okay. To make things worse, she started screaming that she didn't belong here and that she might as well kill herself; her usual modus operandi.

I quickly told my husband to make sure my son stayed in the basement and then had it out with Mother. What I recall so vividly is being acutely aware that I could never help her. I was sobbing and telling her I tried everything my entire life to help her, support her, save her from herself, and that I failed her, and it would never be enough. I told her she should go back home, which shocked her.

What's truly sad about the emotional blow-up I had with Mother is that I never took the time to fully process what I was feeling. I had shut off negative emotions for so long that instead of using this situation as an opportunity for my healing and growth, I buried it, feeling guilty as I called Mother out.

My feelings were valid, and had I stepped towards this crisis instead of moving back, I could have expedited my personal growth years earlier. What's even sadder is Chuck's response, which was a non-response. He heard the entire interchange, including my sobbing, and said nothing.

Obviously, I felt deep hurt and yet never mentioned it. We all did what we trained to do: bury it under the rug. The only consolation was that Mother did not threaten to kill herself again; I had drawn the line in the sand to say I was not playing that manipulation game anymore.

Don't worry, though. Mother had plenty of other manipulation games in her emotional arsenal.

Finally, Mother moved into her condo, which was a total relief. By the end of two weeks, I would have paid anything to get her out of my house. What's really interesting is that at no point did I feel like I was doing anything above and beyond for Mother.

Somewhere during childhood, I had developed the value that, under all circumstances, I must do everything and anything to help the family with zero consideration of the personal ramifications. Guilt, especially when it is hiding below the surface of one's awareness, is a great motivator.

Psychologically, I was an enabling codependent trained to be a parent as a young child, with an overblown sense of responsibility for those in my orbit and a willingness to place my needs behind everyone else's. I never felt betrayed, resentful, sad, or hurt; the emotions I allowed myself to feel were mostly positive, with occasional anger.

✳ ✳ ✳

Recognizing dysfunction is one thing; doing something about it is completely different.

So, Mother got into her routine. We got back into ours, and for a while, things went smoothly. I still wouldn't talk to Mother after 5 p.m. and refused to invite her anywhere in the evening as well. Mother and Chuck's parents had a very interesting relationship, though in retrospect, that's all they had with everyone.

Mother tolerated Chuck's family because Chuck's mom was significantly overweight, and I imagine this elevated Mother. Chuck's mother was also suffering from a huge lack, and what I saw as low self-esteem, so the dysfunction between the two worked. Chuck's parents were always fishing for information about whether we were supporting Mother and whether we purchased the condo, which bothered me for obvious reasons.

From the beginning, Chuck's mother and I weren't in alignment. She coddled my husband and taught him his learned helplessness. While I knew I was on my own and needed to take care of everything or it wouldn't get done, they taught Chuck the exact opposite, which I didn't learn until we were already married, or should I say, I ignored it until I was married.

The things we need to learn about ourselves, we will find in the lessons in others. The problem is that we have to have enough self-awareness to realize that there are lessons to learn. I was aware of everyone else's issues, but couldn't see mine.

As I later told a group of therapists, my issues seem socially acceptable—responsible, hardworking, disciplined, service-oriented, selfless—and they are unless they cross the line into lack of boundaries and enabling, and, therefore, are harder to see.

In simpler terms, I was a giver, and I had surrounded myself with takers, which, sadly, felt familiar—my view of normalcy.

From day one, I felt my mother-in-law was working against me, which was a puzzle. There were always snide remarks that my husband would dismiss, and a sense that she didn't like me, which I found odd since I was working full-time, taking care of virtually everything at home, and handling all family responsibilities with no support.

When my son turned three, we moved firms and then houses. The house we were living in was temporary since we both had a home in CT when we moved to Ohio, and the house we bought would never meet our long-term needs for a larger yard. So we bided our time, and when Kevin was three, we moved firms and used the large sign-on bonus to immediately pay off our house. We never spoke of our money or financial goals, and I was thus taken aback when I heard Chuck's mother say that I was working Chuck too hard and that I would keep moving every few years because of my need for "bigger and better."

None of this was true. We were extremely fiscally responsible, and I was the consummate planner for our financial future, knowing I had no one to back me up. That she said this wasn't the issue. It was that Chuck let her believe this.

Within a short time after my son was due, Chuck's mother started becoming more and more passive-aggressive towards me. When Chuck's sister was around her mother, I would see them exchange glances and smirk, so I knew there was an undercurrent moving against me.

Chuck was mostly oblivious, and when he wasn't, he refused to step in. One incident that really stands out was my first Mother's Day. My sister-in-law called to inform me they were inviting us to Mother's Day, but my brother and partner, who had recently moved to Ohio, were not welcome. Obviously, I wasn't going to go, and Chuck, though he saw the issue, would say nothing to his mother, who continued to run his show.

Coincidentally, they were taking him to the airport for a two-day meeting, and his way of handling it was to tell his mother, "Tricia's furious at you." He refused to take ownership, emotional responsibility, or anything. This became a constant thread throughout our marriage. Even if he admitted to agreeing with me, he wouldn't step in.

The problem is, the less he stepped in, the more passive-aggressive my mother-in-law's behavior became. Mostly, Chuck would say I was overly sensitive, and I just stopped broaching the subject, trying to limit interaction as much as possible. It wasn't until year ten, when Chuck's sister was in alcohol treatment, that I finally felt validated. She called for a two-hour amends call and admitted that she had, out of jealousy, sabotaged me and made up stuff to get her mother to dislike me.

What's so amazing is that many years later, I brought the call up to my sister-in-law, and she had "forgotten" she ever made it.

Chapter 8

You can ignore a problem until it becomes so big that you can't possibly ignore it any longer.

✺

AS LIFE WENT along, Chuck's drinking escalated. He was getting drunk most nights, and I felt like it was affecting my son. I spent every day trying to keep everything afloat and plugging each hole in the dam to keep my family moving in the right direction. It had gotten to the point where I was begging for some more physical help with running our lives. I couldn't keep it all up by myself.

Chuck would feign support, only make it so unbearable that I would just give up in frustration and keep the tasks to myself. What I didn't realize at the time was that I was being manipulated, similarly, as my mother had done my whole life. Later, I came to realize Chuck was barely managing with so little responsibility—again, we were a perfect team, though dysfunctionally stable.

My relationship with my mother-in-law really deteriorated around this time. Chuck had gone out for a business meeting after work, and my in-laws showed up unexpectedly.

I remember feeling so frustrated that I was being forced to entertain them, and then angry because Chuck showed up two hours later than he had promised.

When he finally showed up, he was literally stumbling into the house, drunk, and surprised to see his parents. He was late because he had smashed his car into a pole in the parking lot where he was. Chuck had issues, but he was an exceptional driver, so there was no mistake that he was thoroughly drunk.

I immediately called him out, and my mother-in-law immediately defended him. This was the first time I actually came face-to-face with her enabling behavior so blatantly, and it was shocking. I refused to allow her to revise the truth. I kept telling her, "He is clearly drunk, and he consequently crashed the car." She defended her story and kept throwing out outrageous reasons for what had happened, despite being, under normal circumstances, a bright woman.

This is when I truly realized how deep the problem ran. This was another huge wake-up call I saw and then buried, another wasted opportunity for growth.

Things went downhill from here fast. Both our careers were sailing, but our marriage was sinking fast. I continued to manage everything and tried to micromanage Chuck away from drinking. I really felt like I had four full-time jobs—managing my son's life, career, managing our home life, and trying to keep Chuck sober.

Work was emotionally demanding. I was very good at what I did. In my career, I gave more value than it deserved and more value than I actually cared about, working hard because that was just my programming. I ended up in the financial field because I needed something practical. Because I am better suited for a career in journalism, psychology, or counseling, these skills were an anomaly in finance but actually gave me an incredible advantage. I was tenacious and would fight to the end of the earth for my clients, and this resulted in outstanding success.

I was literally on autopilot. Helping my clients meant everything to me because, subconsciously, I knew I could control the outcome of my business transactions, while my personal life was beyond my control and imploding. There was some comfort in this, which made me very successful.

It was hard not to be on top when my primary goal was to forget the stress of my marriage, not unlike the purpose running served in childhood. Despite my success, I never liked the business. It was simply a means to financial security, which gave me the illusion of feeling emotionally secure.

My husband and I eventually joined businesses, and I continued bringing in clients. Every so often, I would tell him how much I disliked my career. He would never believe me since he did nothing he disliked, so he couldn't fathom that someone else would.

✻ ✻ ✻

*My emotions overload because there is no hand
to hold, there's no shoulder to lean on;
I'm walking on my own.*

My role. Periodically, I would become emotionally overloaded and would have had enough of my life. By now, I was completely oblivious that none of my emotional needs were being met—this felt very familiar to me. What bothered me was how much I was doing, and I had become very resentful that Chuck had so little to contend with compared to me.

Still, every night, he checked out by drinking. It was literally like having a second child. I finally had enough and called EAP (work-provided counseling) and had a counseling session, which was very interesting. I was told that the solution was to stop doing everything, and it would force Chuck to be more responsible. Sounded simple and logical, but in reality, it was not realistic.

Chuck did nothing he didn't like, so yes, it would be off my plate, but not on a plate that would get it done. That I should push responsibilities to Chuck and then detach made sense to the therapist, but in practice, it couldn't work.

Chuck knew what made me tick, and one of those things was a sense of over-responsibility. He knew fully well that I would do whatever he didn't want to do because it would be agonizing for me not to do it. I was essentially being told to let things fall apart, which is something I had tried to prevent my entire life.

In fairness to the therapist, she didn't have enough insight into my history, though perhaps she probably shouldn't have assumed it was a simple solution. Plus, I felt offended; if the solution was that simple, I am fairly certain I would have tried it already, which I had, and it failed.

Chuck was perfectly capable but refused to take on anything that caused him stress; this became more and more of an issue as life got more complicated. In the end, nothing changed, and I simply gave up once again. I was a huge part of the problem, and I couldn't see it since I was trying so hard to keep everything together. I pushed all the blame on Chuck.

Again, we were dysfunctionally stable.

In mid-2003, things got out of control with Chuck's drinking. The more time I spent being successful at work, the less I doted on him, and he started feeling anxious about our relationship. In the end, Chuck wanted the relationship to work. He was so caught up in his own issues that he was incapable of seeing how to make it better.

I became more stressed, and since we worked for the same company, I was concerned that Chuck's drinking behavior would affect my livelihood, which I believed might be my only source of income at some point. We both remained devoted to our son, so one day I asked Chuck to lunch to express how unhappy I was and that things really needed to change. Chuck showed up, falling down drunk.

Apparently, Chuck thought I was going to ask for a divorce or separation, and this is how he handled things. If I didn't know it before this, it became obvious I was completely on my own. A conversation was impossible.

Instead, I drove him to his doctor and told him to get help, or we were done. He moved in with his parents for a while since it was too toxic to have him in the house. This was on a Thursday. By Saturday, he hadn't checked in with our son, and when I called Chuck's parents to tell Chuck he was still a father, his mother told me, "He works out because he's so stressed, and you need to stop pressuring him. He doesn't have a drinking problem at all."

So, this was my life in a nutshell: my mother-in-law defends and enables Chuck's behavior. I try to get him to grow up; guess who always won?

Chuck sought a counselor on my demand; however, he wanted me to go too, which I refused. I felt he needed individual counseling to address his drinking before we could even entertain couples therapy. Another clear warning sign about Chuck was that one day, he was insistent that we go to couples counseling, and when I refused, he somehow manipulated the counselor to come to our home.

Seeing things from where I am today, I see Chuck's primary goal was not to grow and develop himself, but to get me back where he wanted me. He had a pretty nice setup—a nurturing, supportive adult parent who took care of him.

Why would he want to change?

❋ ❋ ❋

> *The Universe is so clever at giving us opportunities,*
> *not necessarily what we want, but definitely*
> *what we need.*

Chuck didn't want to lose me, our son, and the carefully crafted facade we had created, so he actually promised to cut back on drinking. For the interim, he was trying to be on his best behavior, and I was once again hopeful.

Then, I got pregnant with our second son. This was a shock for many reasons: our ages, the age difference between our older and younger son, and the obvious stronghold Chuck would now have on me. Chuck was thrilled, but I knew, at least initially, this meant I wasn't going anywhere. His drinking started up again right where he left off.

My pregnancy went uneventfully, and during the 9 months, I tried really hard to block my unease about my marriage and focus on my newborn son, who was coming. Chuck did not make this easy. His drinking continued, and I didn't have the energy to fight him with everything else on my plate.

My in-laws refused to help me with their son and continued to offer him alcohol every time we visited, as if in defiance. It became a full-time job trying to keep him sober, and I felt like everyone was working against me, and Chuck was mostly oblivious.

Finally, mid-pregnancy, I snapped and had enough. Since Chuck refused to take control of his mother's enabling, and when countless conversations with his parents didn't work, I stopped all communication with his family.

I felt terrible for my son's sake; however, it was not a relationship I could support once they were completely undermining our family. They refused to believe he had a drinking problem, even though I learned that this drinking had gone way back to college to help Chuck with social anxiety. His parents were fully aware of this ever since he was 23; he drove drunk and split his car in two, walked home, and his parents put that story in their vault.

I was also furious with Mother at this point. In retrospect, I was having the stirrings of spiritual awareness, and I decided my relationship with Mother largely set the stage for creating my psychology that allowed me to be attracted to substance abusers and irresponsible people whom I felt responsible for.

I wrote a very candid ten-page letter, never reread it, and sent it; Mother never responded. Whether she ever read it, I don't know. I'm inclined to think she did, but change wasn't happening at this point in her life. Since her entire life was one regret after another, I don't think she could see her role in all our lives.

What she did was give me a handwritten card when my second son was born, letting me know she would help babysit. She and I both knew I would never ask her in a million years to watch my children, ever, but it was a kind gesture.

A couple of weeks before my younger son was born, and months after I had spoken with my in-laws, my mother-in-law called to "make up." She never fully acknowledged her part in any of this, but I didn't want to cheat my younger son out of a relationship, so I went along. Again, no help from Chuck, no revisiting of boundaries, just the usual sweeping it all under the rug as if it never happened.

Work was going great, and any extra time was spent getting things in order for delivery. I was having a planned C-section, so I was as calm as one can be under the circumstances and prepared for a period at home, working where possible. My goals were to spend quality time with my son, keep up with work, and complete the taxes since delivery was in April.

Being pampered, despite the C-section, was not in the cards or in Chuck's way of thinking, and it was definitely not a part of my expectations.

Chuck and I were still working for the same company, so my work logistics were rather easy; I had my computer and my baby, everything was going smoothly, until it wasn't. I planned to manage my accounts from home, and there was one account in particular that another broker tried to steal.

To say this business is the crappiest business ever is an understatement. Like attracts like as far as which clients one works with, but it doesn't insulate you from other unscrupulous people around you. I was on maternity leave, and people were trying to steal my accounts.

Management did nothing. My husband, who was a manager (though in another office), did nothing. Again, I was on my own to fight my battle. Eventually, it became obvious I needed to get back to work to fight for what was mine. I quickly finished the taxes, I had wonderful childcare already arranged, and I went back to work four weeks early.

I complained to management, and their response was to "let me" move to another office. In fairness, my direct manager was extremely accommodating, but he was too weak and fearful of his position to do what was right.

By the time I had been there about a month, and the climate was so adversarial, I knew a change needed to happen. Chuck and I began considering a move to a small regional brokerage firm, and by late 2004 or early 2005, we had switched firms.

Chapter 9

All stress, anxiety, and depression are caused when we ignore who we are and start living to please others.

—Paulo Coelho

※

SWITCHING FIRMS IS never a stress-free experience. This was outrageous. The firm we left was a brokerage owned by a bank, which tried to enforce a non-compete agreement that we had never signed. This was an unbelievable move on their part, very unprecedented considering no contract, and it forced us to sue.

This didn't sit well with my husband, who had fully developed a "need to please everyone" attitude and had zero ability to stick up for himself. We were both being sued. One of us had to take the lead, and my husband literally couldn't handle it. As I saw the foundation of our business suffering, I shifted the focus of the suit to myself.

So, with the suit off his plate, my husband went back to his carefree self, and I took it all on. This was 2005, and things started to become more complicated. Mother's health was failing, which she kept from us, not to shield us from the stress, but so she didn't have to admit her fault in her health demise.

By the time she brought us into the picture, she was very ill. She had worn really baggy clothes, which I later learned was to hide her malnourished body; most likely to her, she looked great because she was "better than all the people who were overweight." What was missing in this equation was that she was drinking herself to death and not taking the pancreatic enzymes she had been told she needed to take for life.

In one of her first of hundreds of doctor appointments over a nine-month span, she told the new doctor that her other doctor had told her she didn't need the enzymes. When the doctor expressed surprise and asked who the doctor was, the mother said, "I don't remember." I caught the doctor's eye and knew exactly what she was thinking.

Lying had been a staple and constant in my entire life with Mother, and you would think I would have been immune by then, but I wasn't. My need to believe in the goodness of Mother far outweighed my intelligence and logic.

This nine-month journey with Mother was another opportunity to grow that I tried to seize but ultimately failed at. For nine months, I spent every day with Mother because it was clear she was dying, even though no one could say specifically from what. MRIs were out because of the many staples in her stomach, but her cancer markers were through the roof. But then again, it could be cirrhosis.

Mother lied nonstop to the doctors about her habits and health, though I missed most of it since she insisted on keeping me in the dark. The biggest lie was that she had stopped drinking, which I found out later. What became apparent is that Mother loved the attention.

Chuck was phenomenal during this period. I couldn't rely on him for the big stuff, but he helped with Mother. Chuck was great as long as I gave him a defined task to do; then he would do it. Just don't expect initiative or empathetic action. Around this time, I appreciated any help, even if I had to ask for it. I was barely keeping my head above water. Chuck put more effort in at work, which I was grateful for while I managed my mother, kids, and home.

My brother stepped in to help as well, for which I was thankful. We had recently moved our office to a new location and needed to hire another sales assistant, and I suggested my brother. My brother is super bright, yet he was never pushed in the right direction, but I felt he would be a trustworthy asset to the office. Chuck was in support of hiring David, which proved to be a very smart decision. I was very grateful for Chuck's support of this decision and still am.

Chuck was amazing at making this happen and pulled every string possible to facilitate this; my brother remains successful at the same firm, promoted many times along the way. This was one of the kindest things Chuck did for me; I will never forget.

Mother's health continued to decline, the lawsuit was getting more contentious, and if I didn't have enough on my plate, we got an audit notice from the IRS stating that we owed a sizable amount of money. Chuck was literally oblivious to it, and in usual form, I took it all on. We had found an obscure tax loophole that we used, and I knew this would complicate the audit. It was legitimate but very unknown.

Because of this, realizing I would end up paying a large amount of money just to get a tax expert up to speed, I fought the audit myself. From August 2005 to March 2006, my life was beyond stressful. I spent my time either taking care of my kids, taking care of Mother, talking to our attorney, researching tax precedent, or trying to keep it all together.

We had phenomenal childcare, which helped tremendously. It got to the point that, since I was juggling it all myself,

I hired a wonderful girl to sit for Ryan, my youngest, on parts of the weekend so that I could tend to everything. During this time, we are also having a large outdoor space installed, which took six months and didn't go smoothly as we had hoped. Overloaded doesn't do justice to how overwhelmed I was.

Mid-fall, early winter, things started going downhill for Mother. She was in the hospital twice, and she was never a compliant patient. On one hand, she loved the attention; on the other, she was dishonest and hated being questioned.

On one such occasion, since she never, ever divulged the extent of her contribution to her demise, doctors were always trying to figure out the puzzle as she presented, wasting tons of money on unnecessary tests. Had Mother told them she was a full-blown alcoholic and that she stopped taking her necessary enzymes, they could have reacted appropriately.

Instead, they were constantly fishing for answers and clues, and Mother conveniently made sure we didn't know when the doctors were visiting. To her, it was one big game, a game she had played her whole life and was quite good at.

Mother was a pro at deception and lying, yet soon enough, the doctors were suspicious. They ended up asking for a psych evaluation, and they concluded that Mother was simply attention-seeking and made herself emaciated to get sick—essentially, a factitious disorder.

Now, this was an incorrect diagnosis. Mother's case wasn't that simple, but I didn't step in because Mother's unwillingness, to be honest, was the cause. Hearing this possible diagnosis made Mother livid since she had essentially disowned any part of her being dependent.

Now, on the one hand, this was accurate. She tried to take care of medical things on her own, but not so much because she was so self-sufficient, more so because she didn't want to be called out on her drinking, as if we didn't know. So Mother's response to the psych evaluation was to get discharged and go home without addressing the situation at all.

Mother claimed that she had no appetite, so every day became a battle to get food into her. I, my brother, or Chuck would drop off six fresh donuts every day—it's what she asked for—that she would "try to eat." Most days, I was told that the donuts would get tossed out due to lack of appetite. Whether the donuts were actually being tossed out was hard to say because months later, I found out from her friend who lived below that he would buy her a sundae each day that she would eat in his presence. Mother continued her manipulation of our emotions and energy. She clearly loved the attention, even if she claimed otherwise.

The cancer markers all pointed to cancer, yet the doctors were at odds trying to figure out where. If she had been healthier or stronger, exploratory surgery would have been done, but for Mother, that was not an option. The lesson I learned here is to never disrespect your body to such a point that it prevents medical intervention. Mother never let on that she caused the mess she was in or that her disregard for her health made it worse.

For me, I had never spent so much time alone with Mother in my life since childhood. Somewhere along the way, I let my guard down and tried to bring up my life to her since she was housebound; this was a tremendous mistake. Never let your guard down with a disordered person, even if it's your mother—a lesson learned for the millionth time.

At first, everything seemed fine, until Mother threw my problems back in my face, emphasizing how petty they were compared to hers. Understanding or empathy was not an expectation, yet I still felt dumbfounded. I was simply trying to bring more life to her, and she was jealous.

It was a huge kick in the stomach and a slap in my face; how dare I think there was room for me to be given to? That wasn't the contract. I needed to give only, and Mother was to receive. For four more months, I visited Mother and never mentioned another thing about my life.

Truth be told, this was fine for her. In my recollection, I don't recall her ever asking about me in my entire life, and later, she never asked about Chuck or my kids. She just didn't care. In reality, she wasn't capable of caring.

Doctors were at the end of their rope and didn't know what else to do for Mother, so they were throwing darts, and the latest was a mammogram. Mother was adamant she didn't have breast cancer. Of course, as they pointed out, she wouldn't know, and they were now doing the process of elimination.

Still, Mother kept me away during her appointments, making me wait outside, presumably so she could lie about what was going on. Privacy laws were in full swing, which I am fairly certain Mother took advantage of, so I was not involved, but I was still trying to save her life. I didn't piece any of this together until much later, though I do recall there always being an undercurrent of dissonance and unease about everything.

The doctors were insistent that Mother needed a mammogram, and they scheduled it for the following week. The night before, I received a frantic call from Mother saying she was in unbearable pain and needed to go to the ER. This was of foremost concern because she was on a morphine, oxycodone, and Neurontin cocktail, so pain shouldn't have been a problem.

We spent several hours in the ER, and the ER doc was livid. Her demeanor and lies did not fool him; he knew she was playing a game, one he had missed. He refused to medicate her further—she wasn't wise enough to realize he had access to everything prescribed.

I was furious because even if she had medication, it wasn't working, and she had a mammogram the same day, since it was now morning. Mother then, with a hint of satisfaction, said, "I guess we will need to cancel the mammogram."

I still wasn't piecing the entire scenario together, but then Mother slipped up. Another doctor came in and asked when she had taken her most recent meds. She stated, "I didn't." She knew she had slipped up. I asked her why she wouldn't have taken the medications, and then she had me take her to the ER in pain.

And then it hit me.

She didn't want to get a mammogram, and she wasn't going. She wasted my time, emotions, the doctors' time, and insurance money; another kick in the stomach. I was really seeing what Mother was capable of and trying hard not to just walk away and tell her she was on her own.

At all times, I felt like I was being undermined, and Mother was working against me. I felt like such a bad person for having these feelings, yet I realized on some level, they were all valid. Still, I was trying to keep my head above water, and, like everything else, I swept it under the rug.

For several months, I didn't know which end was up. My sons were encompassing every free second, as I tried to work, keep home life on track, manage the audit, deal with the lawsuit, and make progress with Mother's health. Mother was visibly failing, but seemed happier than I had ever seen her. I really couldn't gauge where she was emotionally or if she was just so drugged out. She was basically content.

I stopped divulging anything emotionally to her and just focused on her completely; the unwritten contract was, "I am sick, my needs matter. Yours are unimportant." During the nine months I tended to her daily care and the hours we spent together, not once did I express any stress I was going through, and of course, she was unaware of the lawsuit or audit. Why bother telling her? I knew she wasn't capable of caring.

Once in a while, she might inquire about Chuck, but that always seemed to be nosiness as opposed to concern. I told her nothing, knowing she would use it against me. By late November, doctors confirmed Mother was dying and that hospice was to be brought in.

Funny how, after months of failing health and no concrete answer to what was going on with Mother, I felt surprised that hospice had been called. I think the surprise was that I had learned to accept whatever was thrown at me and just assumed this was how my life would be for any foreseeable future. Plus, without a diagnosis, how did they know death was imminent in six months or fewer? My guess is they told Mother more, and she just decided not to share it with me—again, very typical.

I will never forget the day hospice arrived. I was at Mother's condo, waiting, and Mother was acting as if we were waiting for the Welcome Wagon. She seemed almost giddy. I can't say that this was a suicide wish. I think it was more the additional attention she was getting.

Despite forsaking any sign of dependency, it turns out Mother desperately wanted the attention, and it helped shed light on all the years she seemed to hate me due to what I felt were underlying feelings of jealousy. Mother would literally rejoice when something in my life went wrong; her mood and voice would lighten.

For anyone with kids, this is inconceivable. As parents, we all want the very best for our children and are always pulling for them and providing them with a wind. Not Mother.

As we were waiting for hospice that same day, I had another very awkward interaction with Mother. She never gave me advice, never asked about my grades in school, and never praised or complimented me, yet she took every failure as an opportunity to bring me down further. She purposely tried to keep me down when I wanted to get back up and never once offered a hug or said the words, "I love you."

On this day, God knows why, Mother turned on the way out to the patio to smoke and said, "You know I always loved you." Even writing this, I'm still floored, floored because she said it and floored because my only real response should have been, "No!" Instead, I gave her mercy and said, "I know."

In her own demented way, she loved me, but not how a healthy, mature person loves, and the "love" she gave me single-handedly paved the way for every unhealthy way I have allowed others to treat me in the name of that same love. It was wrong then; it is still wrong now.

Hospice came and went uneventfully, only giving us expectations for the next few months. Turns out a big factor in hospice being called in was the doctor's inability to control Mother's pain. Having been in such a compromised health state for so long, her body was not processing pain meds like everyone else. We were told she was taking enough morphine to kill a 270-pound man, and yet it barely lessened her pain.

By now, I was spending hours every week trying to keep her comfortable. There is truly nothing worse than seeing someone you love in total pain and fighting to get something to fix it, or at least to ease the pain.

Because Mother was on such high dosages, it was all a balancing act, and since they were all controlled substances, we could only get exactly what we needed for a month, not one day more, and every month we were fighting, trying to prevent huge lapses in time. Mother complained, and my brother and I jumped through hoops for her.

Now that hospice was involved, things got easier. There's a wonderful place called Kobacker House in Columbus, where Mother spent time for observation so they could get her pain managed without having to sedate her, which they said was a last resort, although I didn't fully understand what this meant until later.

This time was the first time in six months that my brother and I actually had any peace. The staff and volunteers were world-class, compassionate, empathetic, and judgment-free, giving us fourteen days where we could breathe almost normally. During these two weeks, doctors tested many drugs to see what might work, and finally, they seemed to figure it out.

My brother and I went to bring Mother home, feeling the stress come back almost instantly, knowing what we were in for, but it didn't work that way. When we went to pack things up, Mother was playing with the "rabbits that were jumping on her bed" and was quite irate when we could not see them, too. Doctors were called in, and they decided she couldn't go home; she would need to go to a long-term care facility.

I knew this would be both a battle with my mother and a tremendous stress to find a place that would meet her needs, but was relatively close by. We had one week to find a place while she stayed at Kobacher.

In the meantime, the audit, lawsuit, and work were always additional pressure, and I started sensing my husband was drinking more since I was too overwhelmed and distracted with everything else to micromanage him.

Frankly, I had so much other stress besides caring about the safety of my kids. Both were very safe during the days, and when I felt they were at risk, I would hire a babysitter. They both loved to fill in. I was just trying to survive. In seven days, we visited twelve centers. The one we wanted had no vacancies, and then at the last minute, a spot opened up, and we grabbed it. It was considered the best around, beautiful, with all amenities, and it cost a fortune, but we wanted the best for Mother. Then we had to break the news to her.

This didn't go well. Mother loved her condo. It was a haven, and although she never expressed it, I believe it was the first time in her life that she actually had a little peace and happiness.

I felt bad that I wasn't willing to take her in. The doctor didn't think it was possible because of her pain care, but for me, it was because I couldn't subject my boys to her craziness. It concerned me that my kids might lose their innocence the same way I did, so I kept them very isolated from her meanness and drunken rages.

I also knew it was impossible to allocate even one more minute to Mother's care, which was already taking everything I had. So, I basically told Mother this is where she is going, and she has no choice. She ranted and raved, saying she wanted to go home, and I didn't buckle, which was truly a feat.

After hours, she finally relented when I promised to take her home at the first opportunity and that we would care for her cat, Roxanne, which she had failed to realize we had already been doing. Mother was totally so compromised that we were told that she would need an ambulance for the three-mile ride to the center—just another day in our life of chaos.

Finally, Mother was in the care center, but our stress was far from over. The center was one of the best, but it still fell short. As an example, the meds my mother needed to even remotely manage her pain had to be approved by a doctor, and the doctor was hours behind when Mother arrived.

This meant she would be without pain meds for six hours, and worse, she would get behind on the management, which means it would take days to catch up. Nobody cared. Everyone had their own set of problems, so no one's problems were a priority. When meals came, they served Mother what they would term a very liquid, bland meal. This took three days to get straightened out—apparently, someone had said she was toothless and diabetic; neither was true, and one was certainly easy to see. It was clear we still had much to worry about.

Mother had to share a room, and though she seemed oblivious, I could see firsthand the treatment of her bedridden roommate. Yes, the patient was very cantankerous, but from what I saw, the staff was outright mean and borderline abusive. They would yell at the poor lady, roughly move her while making the bed, and threaten to take her food if she wouldn't be quiet—just horrible.

It made me realize my brother and I had to be present still. This was definitely not Kobacker House. I befriended a man across the hall from Mother, who was recovering from a motorcycle accident, and he turned out to be a valuable source of information in terms of Mother's care.

Mother's behavior was getting more extreme. The medical staff blamed it on the drugs. I believe it was the decades of alcohol abuse, coupled with her compromised liver, that were essentially poisoning Mother. They still thought it was pancreatic cancer, even though doctors had removed most of her pancreas decades earlier. The result was the same, so I just let it go.

If not for the man across the hall, I would have never known what was going on with Mother when I wasn't there. It was all kept out of my awareness. Eventually, Mother was moved to a private room.

The new room gave us no peace, but like I said, it was way more pleasant overall, so my brother and I started back to our round-the-clock vigil. I started getting Mother's hair done, which she loved, and really, she was the princess she always wanted to be, well-fed and pampered. Mother was dying, but she had the option to have physiotherapy, and we started seeing her become less compliant and more restless.

Since she was in a private room at this point and way too drugged to be independent and mobile, they placed an alarm under her bedding, so if she tried getting off the bed, the alarm would alert the staff. By now, Mother weighed 85 pounds, was dying from who knows what, if not a disease, probably malnutrition, and nobody attempted to help her eat. It was easier assuming she wasn't hungry.

Food became an enormous challenge because, despite her weight, she seemed to have a ravenous appetite, though she never gained an ounce. A month before, we stopped the donuts because she told the staff, "I don't know why they keep bringing donuts. I hate them." She ate them all, a half dozen each time, but we replaced them with something else. Her cognitive skills were slowly slipping, so Mother seemed not to notice.

The holidays came and went, and though I was managing everything to the best of my ability, there were enormous cracks in my marriage. I was becoming less and less willing to put up with my husband's lack of responsibility, especially as it concerned drinking, and being re-exposed to my mother's behavior and vile attitude triggered everything I had been burying for decades.

In fairness to my husband, this was an unprecedented situation. However, day to day, he did the bare minimum to the extent I never felt like I could let my guard down with him and know he would be sober when I needed him to be.

Work was pressuring him to fill the new office by January, or he would need to move the office to another location. None of this really mattered financially, but it did matter ego-wise to Chuck. What was silly was that he had recruited tons of people, just not to this location, but I learned the image was very important to Chuck.

Where he excelled was in allowing me to do the things I felt necessary for Mother. My constant mantra my entire life has been "no regrets," and caring for Mother, I have none. So for Christmas, we celebrated at home, and then we packed a meal and celebrated at the center. I never knew if Mother appreciated it or not. On her best day, she would never say so, but I know it was a benefit for my boys, and my husband was an enormous help in supporting the effort.

As the new year came, all the stress seemed to mount. Mother's condition was worsening, the lawsuit was picking up steam, and the IRS was pushing to complete its audit. I was literally on maximum overload. My primary aim was just to get through the day.

My husband knew things were not going well between us; however, he seemed incapable of putting my needs above his, so the drinking continued and got worse. The less attentive I was to him, the more he drowned his own demons in alcohol, which meant the more I detached.

We had entered a vicious cycle, which neither of us knew how to stop. In reality, I didn't really care to stop it. I felt very abandoned and used, and it was the first time I actually acknowledged how alone I was and felt, even though I was married.

In mid-January, things took a turn for the worse, which seemed impossible. I was finally settling into bed at around 11 p.m. when the phone rang; I was fully expecting that Mother had passed.

In the few seconds it took to answer the phone, I felt every emotion conceivable, only to find out that someone had passed, but not Mother. I was relieved, thinking the wait was over, but I felt horrible because of the disappointment. I knew Mother would die soon, and each day was a vigil wondering when.

To make things worse, a week later, I received another call, this time at 2 a.m., and again, I assumed Mother had passed. Turns out, Mother was thirsty, and because her drink cart was across the room, she attempted to get out of bed and split her head open badly, and was on the way to the emergency room.

I was so numb from the constant emotional barrage that I didn't act in anger when I found out the center had disconnected her bed alarm because she was so light, and it would go off when it wasn't necessary. Mother tried to get out of bed because no one came. What I felt, though, was total defeat.

The center was the best around, and still, Mother wasn't safe, even at night when she should have been sleeping. This, coupled with how badly I felt for her, just destroyed me. Fortunately, Mother was so drugged up that she didn't feel a thing and was more concerned with her new hairdo being messed up, which says a lot.

I didn't know how much more I could take.

Hospice also saw the gravity of the situation and gave us a break, taking her back to Kobacher for two weeks. We were grateful to have a break, and the center was grateful that we didn't sue them.

March 2005 rolled around, and everything came to a head. On February 25, 2005, I had just left my mother's center, and I received a call from hospice. We had had several conversations over the past few weeks trying to moderate Mother's medication.

Because of her failing overall health and compromised liver, the drugs that were keeping her pain at bay were also causing severe hallucinations, except this time, instead of seeing cute bunnies, mother was seeing evil demons. Mother was literally being tormented every night.

Based on this, hospice informed me they would drug my mother in such a way so she wouldn't be further tormented and that I needed to say anything that needed to be said. To this day, I'm still shocked by this decision. I can't say it was the wrong decision; however, I will say I didn't fully comprehend what they meant until a day later. So I hung up the phone, relayed the information to my brother, went home, made dinner, and went back to Mother.

There really wasn't much to say, regardless. My actions of caring said I loved her, and that was enough for me. We left that night, and when we went back the next day, Mother was essentially in a drug-induced coma. We had discontinued food and water.

It finally sank in.

We were letting Mother die in the most humane way possible. Was this Mother's wish? I couldn't say, since she had been unaware for months. What's so ironic is that during those last several months when she was drugged 24/7, she became kinder and funnier, and I often wonder if this was her true self that she buried long ago.

The doctors expected Mother to pass in the next five to seven days, so my brother and I stepped up our round-the-clock vigil. Chuck tried to help more at home, which allowed me to focus on Mother, or so I thought. In her genuine fighting spirit, Mother did not die in five to seven days as expected. In reality, it took eleven.

On day ten, exhausted beyond belief, I stopped by the office to just have normal human contact, and Chuck was thoroughly drunk. As was typical, he denied it until I looked in every drawer, only to find empty beer bottles.

This was the last thing I needed.

My boys were due to be picked up, and Chuck was supposed to do the picking up. I had to go back to Mother, so it forced me to call my father-in-law to pick up the kids. There weren't enough resources in me to fight. I filed it away for the future and left on such acute anxiety, I'm surprised I was still functioning.

Mother died the next day, March 6, 2006. The IRS settled in my favor a week later, and before the end of March, the lawsuit settled as well. Nine months of hell were over, and somehow, I survived.

I knew I had accomplished a lot, yet I was indifferent to the fact that Chuck didn't even acknowledge it. My concerns were my concerns, and, as usual, he had removed himself from any emotional responsibility for what was going on. This was all I knew, so I accepted this as normal.

Even though I had low expectations for emotional support from Chuck, I was reaching my limit with his drinking. The first few months after Mother's death, I tried to adjust to my new world.

Besides the last nine months of pure stress, it was so odd not to have the burden of Mother hanging over my head. No late-night drunken calls and rages, no more trying to manipulate me for money, no more of my energy needed to boost her up emotionally, no more trying to limit interaction with Mother for emotional protection, and others out of shame—it was very liberating, and I felt a lot of relief and guilt. Relief because I was finally free, guilt because I was relieved. Most people suffer the loss of their parents, particularly their mother, from the perspective of a deep emotional loss of the unconditional love they received and can no longer have.

I didn't have this.

What I felt I believe was akin to a parent who loses an adult child to addiction; I knew this day was coming, and I'm glad it was over, even though you had hoped and prayed for a different outcome. There was zero loss of anything going from Mother to me; this I felt profoundly. Still, I was sad and shocked that when I walked out of the center after Mother had died, my world had changed irreparably, and everyone else was going along, business as usual. My world stopped, but no one else's did. It was very unnerving, and my emotional response surprised me, considering the burden Mother placed on me.

Losing your first parent is never easy. It makes all of us reflect on the limited time we have on this earth. It was the same for me, but worse was the understanding that I would never change Mother. She would never be a loving person, and she would never put my needs above hers, nor would she love me unconditionally.

On some level, I knew all this, and had I been in a better place, Mother's death should have catapulted me towards healing my long-open wounds so I could return to the wholeness that was always there. I didn't take this opportunity; instead, I focused on Chuck's drinking, which was certainly an issue, and jumped headfirst back into life.

Feeling emotions was so detrimental to my survival that pushing them away was what I knew. So I jumped back into life fully until Chuck's drinking became extreme, then I knew something had to be done.

Being emotionally closed off as I was, I didn't feel hurt or abandoned by my husband's lack of emotional support, but was furious at Chuck's lack of presence, mostly for the sake of the kids. My attitude was, "How dare he check out when things get too hard?" I couldn't do that. I am not made that way, so I was always holding up my end and his end, and I was sick and tired.

Chapter 10

If we're holding up our end and theirs, eventually something is going to break from exhaustion.

✹

BY THE FALL of 2006, I had had enough, and finally, in my anger and exasperation, I went to see an attorney. Did I really want a divorce? No, what I wanted, though, was to get off the emotional roller coaster. I longed for normalcy, and I really didn't think about things in the long term. I just felt exhausted being the adult for everyone, while everyone else could be childish and immature. I would rescue them and keep life together, allowing the cycle to continue.

Finally, I decided to hire an attorney and started separation proceedings. In a normal relationship, paperwork would get filed, and the other party served. However, I was not in a "normal" relationship; I was in a codependent relationship, and though I wanted the craziness to end, I didn't feel the power to do so without protecting Chuck at the same time, which is kind of hard if you're suing for divorce.

My goals were to protect our assets and protect my kids. His goal was to protect himself. Because he had brainwashed me into believing that the success of our business was based on a pristine image, I knew Chuck needed to be served unobtrusively. In the end, I told him what was happening, and he went ballistic.

I'm pretty sure Chuck assumed he could do whatever he wanted, and I would never reach my breaking point. After all, his perception was based on how his mother treated him, and I think he assumed I would never give up on him, either. The truth is, I didn't give up on him; I just couldn't put my kids through what I went through.

So, I made an agreement that he would meet the court marshal and get served privately. On the outside, Chuck was a people pleaser. On the inside, he was a manipulator. I never saw this until much later. He played it so well, and I was so blind to it; it was very effective.

Once he was served, and they put holds on our accounts, things really started escalating. Chuck hired a top-notch woman attorney and played the victim like a pro. He got sympathy and ego boost wherever he could, even if it was an outright lie at my expense.

This shed light on what I was dealing with, but I completely missed the magnitude of my contribution to this story.

Oddly, after serving Chuck, the only emotion I consistently felt was relief; finally, no more madness. I started making plans to move forward on my own, and Chuck doubled up his efforts to win me back.

The month Mother died, we had a trip planned to Disney, which we could postpone until September. Although we were separated, we went as a family for the kids' benefit. We had an adjoining suite, so the kids thought nothing of it. Chuck and my son were in one suite, and my other son and I were in another, with the kitchen located between them.

Ironically, this was one of our better trips because Chuck was on his best behavior, and there was no drinking involved, which meant I could relax a minute. Despite the dysfunction, Chuck and I had a lot in common and, if not for his drinking, I felt we shared most major goals and values.

The situation was very sad and not one I ever imagined would happen to me, since I was so aware of the likelihood of being attracted to alcoholics with my past. Still, I wasn't aware enough, and it's the unconscious part of us that often drives our behavior. For all my external planning, my internal world had a different idea.

❋ ❋ ❋

No one is more convincing and more manipulative than an alcoholic hellbent on keeping his safety net.

Chuck was doing everything possible at this point to not have me follow through on our divorce, and most of it was manipulative. He was very strategic in convincing me that if our clients knew we were getting a divorce, our business would be negatively affected. He convinced me not to tell anyone at this point; again, I believed him.

What's so crazy is that I'm not a naïve person, yet when it comes to family and romantic relationships, I was. I trusted way past what I should have and left myself open to being taken advantage of. Leading with empathy and love, I left myself vulnerable, and it worked. In every other aspect of my life, I could stand my ground. With Chuck, I was a puppet on a string, not unlike my relationship with Mother.

We finally made a compromise that Chuck would seek outpatient alcohol treatment and then AA, if I would delay the divorce. I agreed to this, and the following week in October, Chuck entered an all-day weekend treatment program. He would then meet every other day for a few weeks, be required to find a sponsor, and attend AA meetings. This seemed reasonable and certainly worth a try.

Chuck began the treatment that weekend, and I was very hopeful, more so when he showed up at the first meeting completely drunk—this is supposedly common—and the counselor ripped him apart when he tried to use his typical "poor me" victimhood persona.

The therapist, not Chuck, shared this, and for once in eleven years, I thought Chuck and I might make it. It felt good to have someone validate what I was living with.

Chuck really committed himself to the program, at least superficially, and did everything I asked him to do. He found a sponsor and began attending AA meetings. I was also called upon to attend some group meetings in the outpatient program, which perplexed me when the counselors deemed me an enabler. I was, but because I didn't fit the stereotype, I couldn't see it. My perception of an enabler was one who was essentially a doormat and walked all over. This was more indicative of my mother-in-law. I was feisty, complained, and tried to change Chuck's behavior, believing that if he changed, our relationship would change.

What I didn't understand was that if I didn't change as well, things would never fully improve. I erroneously believed that once Chuck stopped drinking, he would step up to the plate as both a father and a husband. I never heard the term "dry drunk," but I would soon understand what that meant.

After outpatient treatment, Chuck seemed to commit himself to AA, and the divorce was called off. I assumed he was a man of his word and stopped drinking, so I never questioned that. As time wore on, the euphoria that he originally experienced when he got sober wore off, and, as an introvert, though he never was forcibly mean, Chuck became more reclusive and quiet.

Since he was an introvert, this didn't concern me, but what did concern me was that he seemed to be more and more affected by the stock market each day. I could tell you what the stock market did just by the look on his face each day: on a good day, he was happy; on a bad day, we needed to leave him alone.

Chuck's behavior seemed to have become more regimented, yet even then, I didn't recognize the implications. I was simply grateful I could ask him to drive the kids somewhere, and he would be sober.

Chapter 11

*Sometimes we find our way when we get out
of our own way and let life happen.*

✺

OUR RELATIONSHIP GOT no closer. This was both our fault, and I still continued to do the majority of the tasks, but again, life was so much less chaotic, so it worked for me. Ryan was now in school, and after a mild hiccup at the standard public school, we moved him into the progressive public school's first-grade class, and this literally changed all our lives.

My son struggled with the regimen of contemporary education, but with the more thematic approach at the progressive school, he flourished, and I found my tribe. Having come from such a unique background and mindset, it didn't detach me from my community, but I never felt like I found people with whom I could connect.

The progressive school attracted a particular parental mindset, and for the first time in my life, I found people I could relate to. This was the beginning of a significant spiritual transformation for me, even though I didn't realize it at the time.

For the next several years, while my younger son was in elementary school, I completely immersed myself in volunteering as a fundraiser chair and really felt like I was finding myself. I continued volunteering with my older son's sports teams, organized community volunteering events, and, for the first time in my life, felt a little more than content.

I was still handling most of the tasks at home and carrying too much of everything, but compared to before and the past stresses, things were going well. My husband handled the maintenance of our business, and mostly, I didn't worry too much about our finances. We seemed to hum along.

And then 2008 came, and everything changed again. I started paying a bit more attention to our finances because, after completing our taxes, I realized that my husband had made approximately one thousand trades, and in the end, we lost money. I was resentful of having to type each transaction, and even more resentful when it was a loss. I started sensing a pattern and really paying closer attention to our accounts. We had always lived significantly below our means and saved a lot of money each month, so up to now, money worries were not on my radar.

In the past, whenever there were enormous drops on our accounts, Chuck would convince me it was a movement between accounts, and we had so many that it was quite possible. When I started questioning him this time, he became very agitated, and I realized this was more of an issue than I had realized.

❋ ❋ ❋

It takes trust and vulnerability to give someone full access to your finances. Better make sure your values are in alignment.

We started having weekly battles about our finances, which then turned into daily ones. The stress of our finances replaced the stress I felt with Chuck's drinking. I was always a very conservative investor and liked the fact that he was as well, so his behavior with our account was surprising and concerning. He would do a transaction, lose fifty thousand, and not bat an eye, believing he could make it back the next day.

Chuck was a very solid stock trader, having worked on a trading desk before going into the client side of finance, so he was considerably better than average. The problem was he didn't seem to grasp that it was both real money and not all his to play with. He was taking enormous gambles, and often with our retirement accounts and our joint account.

This was our career, and yet as the market was going up, the two people with the most knowledge were having our accounts go down. This was such a huge stress in our home because, as I was slowly becoming more conscious, I realized the depth of value I had placed on money as a means of emotional security, having grown up with so little and fully on my own since I was seventeen. Taking unnecessary gambles made no sense to me.

Worse was that Chuck never seemed to learn his lesson. In 2000 and 2001, Chuck had grown our account to such a level that, if we had never saved another penny and just averaged a five percent return, we could have retired at fifty-five and had enough money long after we were gone. He never got out, and we lost the majority of it.

I blame this on his newness on the retail side of business and on the fact that the tech bust was an anomaly. Regardless, Chuck knew my risk tolerance and how much anxiety this caused, and claimed to have respected where I was with our finances. In the years following the tech bust, I orchestrated some huge career moves, both of which benefited Chuck and our family, less for me and more to bail out our finances with what he had lost.

Chuck behaving irresponsibly with our money, me finding out, and him apologizing and swearing to never do it again became a constant cycle. Watching Chuck do the same thing all over again was a kick in my face and very hurtful; although in those days, my hurt translated into anger.

Things had gotten so bad that I even had him sign a written agreement stating that he would stop his trading behavior and would not make any further option trades without mutual agreement. This came after I threatened to move the account to another broker, and he claimed the embarrassment would ruin his career. Manipulated again.

September 2008. The country was just beginning its financial crisis, although no one had any idea how bad it was going to get. In March, the federal government bailed out Bear Stearns, which should have been a huge wake-up call that something was amiss for the government to have intervened.

Chuck was never one to change direction without a huge push, and this was not big enough to get him to stop doing uncovered options on margin, which could really ruin us financially. To him, this is what he knew, this is what he liked, and this is what he was going to stick with.

I was very familiar with how options worked, but I was kept largely in the dark about the margin account and the amount of exposure we had to market risk.

Then, Lehman Brothers was on the brink of collapse on September 14, 2008. I was hyper-focused on our account, wanting to believe in my husband, but also not wanting to be destitute.

I recall watching *Fast Money* that afternoon and hearing about an option that, if put together correctly, we could only make money, a kind of once-in-a-lifetime opportunity. Immediately, I called Chuck because by then, I had forbidden him to do any options in our account without asking. He also saw the segment and agreed it was a fantastic opportunity to make up for what we lost. We invested a huge chunk and waited until the next day, when the options would expire.

The next day arrived, and in an unprecedented decision, the government did not bail out Lehman, and it filed for bankruptcy. This was great news for us because with the option strategy, we would make a ton of money back. Finally, Chuck and I agreed!

During the next part of the morning, I tried to reach Chuck so we could celebrate together, and each time, he was on the phone, which made me angry since I thought he would want to share the success with the person who suggested it. I thought he was probably celebrating with the clients he did the same transaction with.

Finally, I was getting perturbed and said I would hold until he answered. It turned out that he was actually avoiding me. His ego got the best of him, and instead of sticking to the plan we had agreed upon, he became greedy and thought he could make twice as much if the government bailed out Lehman. So, he took half the trade-off, losing $125,000 when the company went bankrupt.

When I saw the financial damage my husband had done, I should have been more aware of the "why" he did what he did. Instead, my anger and then utter frustration took over. This wasn't the first time Chuck had broken a promise, and it wouldn't be the last, but this had no room for any misinterpretation of what we had agreed on. He couldn't gaslight his way out of it, though back then, I had no inkling what gaslighting even meant.

Chuck was remorseful, but remorseful couldn't bring back $125,000!

So, as always, I dug in, and it took four days until I came up with a plan to bail us out. Chuck was adamant that he could make it back, and a part of me wanted to believe him. I wish I weren't so naïve and trusting.

Finally, we came up with an agreement. Chuck would "day trade" a portion of our money, and I would invest the rest in something more conservative with a guaranteed return. Chuck promised to run every transaction by me and agreed that once the account was whole, he would stop trading; we would then move the money into something more conservative.

I would like to say he honored his word, but he didn't, and it wasn't until a few years later that he told me he had gotten us back to the hole in early 2010, only to bury us again. There were so many red flags with his behavior, but by now, I was up to my neck in codependency, and every day was just trying to keep the illusion of control going.

By 2012, we had lost so much money that it seemed impossible to believe he wouldn't stop. He thought through all his trades, but he always got greedy and was always on a whale hunt for the biggest whale he could find.

The stress was so much that at some point, I stopped looking at the accounts. The balances oscillated by huge swings each day, and the way options were priced was very confusing. Chuck would always say enough to make me relax and think he had things under control.

Money was always the biggest source of conflict for us, not unlike many couples. However, unlike many couples, we never fought over our respective spending habits. We were both frugal. We both contributed equally, so that was never a problem either. The only problem was our investment style.

I am risk-averse and would be happy with less to avoid the difficulties of the market, and Chuck was a thrill seeker and, as I came to realize later, loved the "adrenaline rush" of a brilliant trade. The risk was never worth it to me.

In 2013, we started making a little back, but we were now hovering around one million dollars in losses. As avid savers and high earners, we always had plenty of savings. However, the figure literally made me sick to my stomach daily. I just couldn't fathom how Chuck could allow this to escalate so far out of control. Trusting an addict is never smart.

Chuck used many strategies to keep me on board, and most I ignored and didn't allow him to manipulate me. One day, though, he told me at the worst of it in 2012, he had considered jumping off a building. Chuck was not above using any tactic possible to get me back in his corner, and this worked. I asked if he was serious.

He was noncommittal, but after my childhood, it was the wrong manipulation to use. I was very vexed that he would even attempt to use the threat of suicide as a manipulation strategy, and I told him that if he ever went down that road again, to make me feel bad for him, I would leave. I had terrible boundaries most of my life, but this was a line-crosser, even for me. Oddly, Chuck seemed shocked by my reaction, again, a huge red flag on his emotional detachment.

When I started meeting people at Wickliffe, my son's elementary school, an entirely new world opened up. I began seeing myself differently, recognizing that I resonated more with the people who live life purposefully, with meaning and passion.

This was foreign to me, considering the people I had come into contact with so far. I was always an anomaly in the brokerage business, and I resonated more with the support staff than with the brokers. The business rewards those who are doing the most business, without regard for who's serving their clients ethically.

I was always feeling offended and struggled to keep my mouth shut since my husband managed the office. Chuck was great at compartmentalizing things, so he could operate in that environment with little psychological distress.

I could not.

It bothered me on the deepest level, and at some point, I started working from home to survive. When I started meeting people at Wickliffe, everything began making sense. I still wasn't able to see things in their entirety, but I could no longer push down my inner feelings of unrest.

Chapter 12

*Try as we might, once we feel "seen," it is
hard to go back to being "unseen."*

✹

I HAVE ALWAYS BEEN service-minded and other-centered, especially toward those less fortunate, but now my focus has shifted predominantly to helping others. My true self was begging to come out, though I didn't see it as such, having spent decades living behind a mask to survive.

Every path we take shows us more about who we are if we choose to see it. I was changing, but it was happening imperceptibly as opposed to a conscious decision. Some say that we attract people at the exact emotional level we are at, much like the pull of a magnet. Within a couple of years, Chuck's and my magnets were no longer matching up.

Again, I wasn't aware enough at the time to know what was happening. I just knew something was happening. A few very important people crossed paths with similar stories of childhood trauma, and hearing them tell their stories with such vulnerability made it safe for me to tell my story that I had buried in a mountain of shame for so long.

I have since learned that when you feel a pull toward someone, go toward them. There is usually a lesson to learn, or they are there to help us see things we cannot see on our own. People we feel a magnetic pull toward, man or woman, have the power to help us grow exponentially; I only wish I had known this sooner.

As I grew, my relationship with my husband grew apart. Looking back, things unfolded in a way that I missed the nuances of everyday life and how they affected our marriage. What we lacked in emotional intimacy, we made up for with our shared love of family traditions and our kids. We never missed an event. We hosted holidays, traveled, and volunteered together for numerous organizations. On the surface, everything looked great; underneath, not so much.

Sadly, we were in such a holding pattern that neither of us saw what was festering below the surface. Chuck was still up to his shenanigans with our finances, but I had grown resolved to the fact that I needed to trust him because, otherwise, stress overload would consume me. Sadly, he saw this as an open door, and things got worse.

Life was still as chaotic as ever, and I had become so accustomed to handling everything on my own that I continued down this path, never thinking there was another option.

When an IRS agent showed up at my door—they might not call, but they could visit your home—I didn't even tell Chuck. I knew he would react poorly to the stress of it, and it was less stressful for me to just handle it by myself. I called a friend who put me in touch with a tax attorney, who advised me on what to do. I did it, and eventually it went away. My husband was none the wiser.

When I was told by my younger son's first-grade teacher that my son was excelling academically, but in her words, as she pounded the table with her finger, "There's something wrong with him," I researched an educational psychologist, took my son to the appointments, and consulted with the psychologist.

When I was told my son felt bored and, for self-esteem reasons, we should send him to the progressive school immediately, I wrote the letters to the district and orchestrated the transfers.

When we tried getting my son into the public middle school, which was not in our district, we were told no, and I fought the battle alone as well. I petitioned the school board, presented my case, and they turned me down, but I knew I had a legal right to my request. So, I presented my case again, and eventually, they relented.

Like most families, things happen. In my family, I knew my husband couldn't handle the stress of anything, particularly if there was conflict, which might make him look poorly, so it fell to me. The stress of involving him was greater than the stress of handling it myself.

I took it like a champ. Truthfully, on most days, I didn't even realize how unfair things had gotten. I was just living the path I knew since I was six and a half years old. Other than the mandatory people that needed to be involved, the entire world could be crashing around me, and you would never know by my demeanor.

I was under high stress all the time. Like the frog in the boiling water who starts in a cold pot that slowly heats, so it never jumps out, I never saw how stressed I was. In reality, the signs were all there, but I mostly ignored them. There were months on end that I didn't sleep, lying next to my husband, who would fall asleep in minutes.

In retrospect, of course, he did. I carried all the problems. He was free as a bird. Some nights, I was so stressed that I would go into our brokerage accounts, see the carnage, and my heart would be literally racing. At these times, I would wake him up and try to make him explain what he was doing, practically begging him to make me feel better. He never did.

Instead, he would shut down or, worse, tell me to let him sleep so he could be better prepared to make back the money, and he promised that he would discuss it once he got to work. Everything was an avoidance tactic, and the discussion inevitably never happened. The anger just got buried even further, and resentment became my go-to emotion.

In fairness, we were both operating from a belief system that was instilled in us decades before that created a story about our lives that wasn't true. The problem is, it was so ingrained, it felt real. I learned from childhood to do what's necessary, whether I liked it or not; Chuck learned he only needed to do what he liked. We were just playing the role we were taught, and we both played it well. I not only enabled my husband, but I was an equal opportunity enabler, so my kids got the same behavior from me—my older son, more so, and I was his wind for far too long. I had very little support growing up and no modeling for positive parenting, so I was often improvising, although I think most parents can say the same.

I had poor boundaries, and I sheltered him from as much emotional hardship as possible. If they didn't make a sports team, the coach was called, and we got him on another team that increased our drive by one and a half hours every night just so he didn't have to experience emotional pain. If he got overlooked for something at school, I would make a call to ask why.

We encouraged and supported friendships beyond belief; exceptional grades were expected, and we proofread papers until they were perfect. We donated time and conducted fundraisers for his sports teams. I was all-in as a parent, and it wasn't until future events happened that I realized what a detriment this behavior was.

I know I tried my best, and I loved my sons unconditionally, so they are fine young men. But from today's perspective, I think I could have done better. We can't erase the past, so I focus on the present and future, but I'm fully aware that even when we try our best, we can still fall short. Once we are aware, it's much easier to see where better choices could have been made.

My focus as a parent was to make sure both kids knew how we loved them, but also had a deep sense of gratitude for the privileges they had as well as a dedication to service to others. I actively tried to mitigate the pressures of entitlement growing up privileged in a town where entitlement is rampant.

Mostly, I did a decent job at this, but still, I know I could have done better if I had known better. My journey from childhood has now become part of their journey that they will need to overcome. What we don't heal, we will repeat.

✵ ✵ ✵

Denial is an amazing defense. You can deny the truth, but it doesn't make the truth go away, and eventually, the truth will make itself known and won't always be pleasant.

As my older son progressed through high school, life never fully settled down, but it was a really fun period for our family. My younger son was doing great at the progressive school, and my older son was a superstar at his school. The focus and attention we put on our kids were unlimited, so it was the marriage that suffered.

I started growing more spiritually and was becoming very disillusioned with the marriage. I still loved my husband. You love what you take care of, and I took care of him. I was always his biggest fan, listening to his problems, offering advice about the office, and trying to make him happy. Other than the periodic financial blowups, things weren't too bad during this period. However, I was becoming more aware of the psychology behind who I had married.

Basically, I realized I had married someone with my mother's and stepfather's psychology.

Did I consciously acknowledge this? No, but on some level, I knew. At various points during my older son's high school years, the multitude I was managing overwhelmed me, and I would often beg my husband to take over something. He would agree to take over on a specific date, which never came, or, as I figured out years later, his best strategy was to overwhelm me with minute, detailed questions about the history. It was so overwhelming that I would give up out of frustration.

He could have just taken it over and asked along the way, but he had no desire or intention to do so. Chuck knew exactly which buttons to push to get his way, and it always worked. Eventually, he would stress me out so much that it was easier to do the task myself.

During this period, I started having what I call "mini breakdowns." In my marriage, I cried only a few times, and always on occasions like funerals. I never cried day to day, I never felt sorry for myself, I never acknowledged my hurt, I never gave up, and I never acted hopeless—I never learned this in childhood.

In fact, I could never experience these feelings, period. Every once in a while, I would wake up in the morning and feel the deepest sadness I have ever felt. I can recall feeling this way a few times, and each time, Chuck would look at me and wonder what he was supposed to do. He was the taker, not the giver, and he had no clue how to comfort the rock. He would ask me what he could do, and through my deep sobbing, I would say, "I don't know," and "I am deeply unhappy."

And I was. I was so unhappy, and these moments were like the emotional dam breaking open and releasing all my pent-up hurt and sorrow. These were monumental red flags that something was drastically wrong.

It would freak Chuck out, but it also freaked me out. I was so used to keeping it all together that this flood of emotion was so unnatural and difficult for me to process. This would last ten minutes, and then I would compose myself. Chuck would go to work. I would do the same, and neither of us would mention the incident until the next time.

Years of heartache could have been avoided had I taken the opportunity to question what was going on. My true self was begging to be seen. This was a missed opportunity from my Soul; I just wasn't ready.

My older son's final year at high school was busy for him and busy for me; life was truly a whirlwind. Between all my other responsibilities, I spent hours helping my son with college essays, applications, scholarships, and a multitude of dances, proms, and events. Life was as full as it could be. I was splitting at the edges, but so grateful that my son was turning into such a fine young man.

Previous to this, our church went on a mission trip during spring break to build homes in Tecate, Mexico. And we had decided years before that we would go as a family, including our younger son, for whom they made an age exception. We were so excited to share this amazing service experience, possibly for the last time as a complete family. Little did we know how prophetic this would be.

Going to Tecate, Mexico, in March is always a challenge. The days can reach 90°F, and the nights drop into the 20s, making packing both labor-intensive and arduous. We sleep in tents all week without showers or electricity, relying on outhouses and with luggage limitations of 50 pounds. Packing for this trip took hours.

For five days, we worked at construction sites all day, exhausted yet exhilarated by a shared experience with 75 other adults and high school students. Many things happened on this trip that made an indelible mark on me.

The first was when we set up our tent. I have never been a fan of reading directions, and although I made sure all the parts were in the duffel, I didn't follow the mission leaders' advice to set up the tent ahead of time. My assumption is that I am someone who can figure everything out. This would be no different.

Well, setting up the tent did not go as easily as planned. In fairness to the tent company, it was easy. It's just that it required two people, and my husband's usual defense when he might have to stretch is to blame and give up.

He did both.

He blamed me for not setting up the tent beforehand, and no, he didn't see how ludicrous it was that he hadn't. Then, he essentially wouldn't help. We were the last tent up. My older son looked mortified, and luckily, a soon-to-be good friend swooped in and set it up in minutes.

The scenario did not embarrass me, but it made me realize how unsupported I was and how I handled every task, even the ones that every other man at camp was doing. We enjoyed the trip, but barely interacted.

Chapter 13

*When you don't know who you are, how can
you expect someone else to know you?*

✸

LITTLE BY LITTLE, over the course of twenty years, my free-spirited self was chipped away and lost, replaced by a Type A, hard-charging, get-it-done woman. Admittedly, I was just beginning to discover my true self when I met Chuck, and, unfortunately, as a people pleaser, it was easy for Chuck to mold me into what he wanted.

My boundaries were weak, a leftover from childhood, and I was no match for my husband, who was a pro at manipulation. He was so good that it wasn't until much later that I really understood that I had replicated my childhood in my marriage.

By the time we got back from our family mission trip, a trip that really affected me on a spiritual level, if not consciously, I was transforming. What this meant was that I was becoming increasingly intolerant of being taken advantage of. I started challenging my husband's behavior more and more, especially when it related to his management of our money.

Around this time, the oil industry was bombing, and my husband, being a contrarian investor, purchased oil stocks as everyone was selling them. Many arguments arose from the contrast in our investment styles, and I remember asking him repeatedly why he thought he was smarter than everyone else on Wall Street. Chuck would promise to stop, but then lie about making stock trades. The stress he was causing me was unbearable, yet he would continue doing what he wanted.

Chuck knew he could get away with this because he always presented a picture of honesty, and I bought the picture. The truth is, he wasn't honest with himself, so how could he be honest with me?

Despite all that I had gone through in my life, this period was perhaps the most stressful. I never felt enamored with the brokerage industry, particularly the day-to-day stock picking. However, to protect our future, I had to stop the steady decline. This meant I was having to seek stock ideas, often for eight hours a day. This caused me so much stress, and I thought I would have a nervous breakdown. Imagine watching your entire life savings disintegrate and my sense of security right along with it.

Savings afforded me emotional safety, which in retrospect was very misguided but very real. I was so desperate to stop the monetary bleed from progressing while Chuck was on the other end, hiding trades and the monumental losses. I wanted to believe in his abilities more than anything.

By October 2015, I could no longer take the stress. I hadn't slept in months while he continued to sleep peacefully, and I knew, for my health, I needed to detach from the mess my husband had made. So, Chuck and I sat down to discuss my line in the sand. I made him promise to only purchase blue-chip stocks that paid dividends, and anything speculative, he would run by me. I again believed him. He was amazing at telling me what I needed to hear, and I tried to regroup and mitigate my overwhelming sense of dread and stress. Besides these promises, I also made Chuck acknowledge that if he lied again, he was to move out. He agreed.

Between Christmas 2015 and New Year's 2016, we spent a leisurely week in New York City, visiting family and just having a chill time together. Kevin was home from college, and we thought this might help loosen some of the tension in the household.

During this week, Chuck was very distant and not engaged at all, spending an inordinate amount of time watching the stock market channel. At one point, I was so annoyed by his detachment that I asked him to leave if he couldn't be more attentive to the family. To his credit, he tried. Little did I know what he was actually dealing with.

For the entire seven days, I blocked out the family stress, primarily our financial stress, and just focused on having fun with the family. We watched the ball drop in Times Square on a surprisingly warm New Year's Eve, and for a minute, I was very hopeful we could fix where Chuck and I had landed, not unlike the hope my parents probably felt when they had their new house built. Little did I know that this was actually the beginning of the end, ironically, just like my parents.

By January 2016, things settled back into a normal pace, and since Kevin was home from college, I focused on him and being a family again. Kevin returned to college at the end of January, and I got back involved with our finances, only to find out Chuck had not honored a single thing he had agreed on and that, in fact, our account had dropped by $100,000 more.

I cried, which was very unusual back then, and when Chuck got home, I asked him to leave. He tried to appeal to my emotions, but I had finally had enough, and I wouldn't allow him to sway me this time. He went to stay with his father, which wasn't a terrible move since his father was 87 at the time and could use the support.

In the end, I didn't really want to end our marriage. I just wanted the madness to end. I finally recognized that it was never going to end because Chuck didn't seem to care about the stress he was causing me, and my guess is that he felt I would calm down and welcome him back in the end.

This time was different, though. I had actually had enough.

Every day, I was sick and tired of how I felt, of the lack of emotional support Chuck gave me, and of the fact that I took care of every aspect of our lives, while he continued to blow up our future. I later learned he had an addiction to the rush of the stock market, but when you're in the middle of the chaos, it is very difficult to see the truth.

Life progressed for a while, and each day, I felt more resolute that I wouldn't return to the same marriage, if at all. Chuck continued to act as if nothing was wrong—told no one that we had separated, continued to coach my younger son's basketball games, and occasionally would stop over for dinner with Ryan and me.

Periodically, Chuck would literally beg to move back in, and though I missed him on some level, I didn't miss the stress. Sadly, without him in the house, nothing had really changed. I had been doing 100 percent of everything, so his absence was minimal. The kids knew we were having problems, and even they just accepted it.

After all, no one's life had really changed. In the end, that is one of the saddest statements. Nothing really changed.

Chapter 14

Do we ever really know what someone else is thinking, or is it only our own projections we see? Do we ever really know someone?

❋

IT IS MY impression that there are events in our lives that, if we choose to notice, send us on a different path. The first time this happened to me was when I was six and a half and Mother attempted suicide. The second time was when I stood up to Stepfather, and he never attempted to touch me again. The third was meeting my husband on a blind date at work at a job that literally fell in my lap, and the last was on February 8, 2016. There were many smaller benchmarks, but these are the ones that caused enormous shifts in perspective and life circumstances and allowed for the most potential for growth.

We often view life as a random series of events and choices that lead us to where we end up. Although we always have free will, I contend that some choices are better than others and usually facilitate the greatest opportunity to raise one's consciousness.

Literally, until February 8, 2016, I shielded my husband from the consequences of every action he took. I did it out of a distorted sense of love I learned from my childhood, and I see now how wrong it was.

I didn't let my husband suffer the consequences of his poor choices and the discomfort that came with them, and consequently, he never learned not to repeat the behavior and never grew. This was the legacy from his childhood, and we worked amazingly well together, though dysfunctionally. This would have gone on forever, except I was no longer willing to play my role.

Without realizing it, I was tired of giving everything and getting minimal in return. I was changing the unspoken contract Chuck and I made 21 years earlier.

Something happened at work that threatened Chuck's 35-year impeccable career and image, and he called me that day to say, "You have to handle this." For the first time in our marriage, I said, "No."

Not only did I refuse to handle it, but I really didn't want to be a part of it. I felt it to be extremely selfish that Chuck dragged me into his drama when I had nothing to do with it, and we had technically separated.

The truth is, I couldn't fix his problem. It would have to play out, but what he really wanted was for me to take on the emotional stress of it as I had done for 21 years, and as customary. In my mind, I wasn't even doing "tough love." I simply had had enough. This both shocked Chuck and sent him into a tailspin. He did not have the emotional resilience to handle anything, much less something that threatened his pristine image.

Over the next week and a half, it took all my willpower not to step in and help Chuck, especially when I saw him sink even deeper into the stress of the situation. While I felt bad, I honestly believed that this could be the turning point in our marriage; he would need to step up to the plate on his own, and he would realize he was not as helpless as he felt.

I never voiced this to my husband. In fact, I took a very hard stance, realizing that any encouragement from my coming back if he stepped onto the plate was counterproductive. I knew Chuck needed to prove to himself that he could fully handle this situation, and not just to get me back.

Mostly, I kept a very distant stance regarding his actions as he tried to deal with what was happening. I firmly believed he was strong enough to handle this on his own.

The problem itself was absolutely minimal in the entire scheme of things, but to him, since it threatened his perfect image, it was monumental. Many strange things happened over the next two weeks that seemed like an overreaction on his part.

Chuck's mood at this time oscillated between acceptance and helplessness. On the days when he had acceptance, he was very productive and tried to "protect us," although in very erratic ways. For example, he moved all the accounts into my name and removed himself from the deed to the house in case he was sued.

None of his behavior was rational, and I argued against the validity of all his actions, ignoring his ridiculousness, even if it was counterproductive. I have chalked it up to him trying to prove to me he wasn't as financially careless as I thought.

My brother was keeping tabs on him at work, and based on his behavior, I had a sense that he was doing fine, or at least marginally better. Chuck stayed engaged with Ryan, and we still shared dinner where it made sense. I was feeling like maybe we could get back to some form of equilibrium, but every time I thought that, Chuck would say something that would make that less of a possibility. By now, I was realizing and beginning to experience my emotions, and was feeling very "cheated" in my marriage.

PANEL THREE

Rewriting the Story

*The unraveling. The return.
The quiet remembrance of who I truly am.*

Chapter 1

*Sometimes things have to fall completely apart
before it's possible to put things back together.*

✸

IN EVERYONE'S LIFE, some events have the power to redirect our journey. Sometimes these events are common stages of life: kids go off to college or a parent dies. At other times, these events are less predictable, such as a "surprise" divorce or a chronic illness.

These events are opportunities for us to reflect on our lives and decide if we are living in balance with our deepest hopes and dreams. We can choose to take on these Soul challenges, or we can choose to overlook them.

And then there are challenges and events that completely obliterate everything we ever knew to be true. We feel as though we have been shot out of a canyon with all the pieces of our inner being blown into a million pieces, and no matter how hard we try, we can't put ourselves back together the way we were before. The latter happened to me, and my life would never be the same.

On February 21, 2016, a knock on my door woke me at 1:10 a.m. to find four police officers standing at my door. My older son was at college, and a mother's usual instinct was, "What happened to my son?" But without asking, I knew they were there because of my husband.

The police officers told me that my husband had taken his life at his office, jumping from the sixth floor to his death. For the next one and a half hours, I screamed in a ball on the kitchen floor while these very patient police officers waited until I was done. Blessedly, my 11-year-old never woke up.

From there, everything was surreal. Police deem all suicides homicides until proven otherwise, and because of the manner of my husband's death, his was very questionable. In my heart, I knew my husband had taken his life, but I let the officers interrogate me until they felt satisfied. I was told to call someone so I wasn't alone, and it took me at least twenty tries to remember how to use my phone.

I couldn't reach my brother, and they finally sent police officers to his home to let him know. These were the longest and shortest six hours of my life. Shock got me through it, and, in retrospect, the dissociation I needed to survive my childhood made me uniquely prepared for this trauma.

I finally got everyone to leave and got my son up without mentioning what had happened, knowing I needed my older son to be home first. I made breakfast, packed his lunch, and drove him to school, as if it were just another day.

✸ ✸ ✸

*Someone can do the unthinkable to save themselves,
yet destroy everyone else in the process.*

The night of Chuck's death, we had what would prove to be our last conversation. That evening, I recall sitting in our church parking lot before a youth group, where I was a leader, and Chuck told me another version of what was going on at work and in our accounts.

This was approximately the tenth version in two weeks, and I just couldn't take it a minute longer. The last thing I said to him was, "I don't think we were going to make it," and he said, "I know," and we hung up.

Before the last interchange, assuming he was home with his father, I told him to come clean to someone, and his father would be a good option since he was available. I knew I had no more to offer him emotionally at this point.

It turns out he wasn't home, but he was at the office. I later found out that he did indeed call his dad and even went as far as saying he was going to take his life and to please look out for me and the kids. My father-in-law gave him advice to essentially "man up" and sadly went to bed. He, too, woke up a bit later and, reflecting on the conversation, tried calling Chuck in case he might be suicidal. He never reached him, probably assuming he was overreacting and went back to bed. But by then, it was too late.

The problem with suicide is that for those of us who do not have this as an option in our repertoire of options, it's inconceivable that it could be an option for someone else. Looking back, Chuck's behavior showed suicidal ideation and possible intent.

However, at that point, I was very ill-equipped to even know the language or actions of a suicidal person. Couple that with the fact that I dealt with Mother using suicide threats to manipulate me for so long, and I wasn't at all in tune with what someone else might actually do.

Looking back, there were so many red flags. Chuck was afraid of getting sued, so he started putting everything into my name. His logic was off because I knew it was all traceable, and I expressed this to him, but he seemed hellbent on doing it until I finally gave up.

Chuck was under severe stress that was clear in his body language, and then four days before his death, he calmed down, right back to his calm state. He asked to have dinner with me the night before. We did, and he told another version of what was going on, which is what prompted my reaction the next night.

Somewhere in the week he died, he expressed to me that now I could "go back to being your free spirit." I assumed he meant because of divorce, and I was actually quite resentful that he was aware he was complicit in taking that away from me.

He had a therapy appointment set for the Monday before he died, and prior to going in, he called to say he felt he should wait until after his problem at work was resolved, so there wouldn't be a mental health record. It sounded logical and well thought out.

He took my son and dog on a walk five hours before his death and told my son they would start bird watching together. Nothing seemed out of the ordinary in real time, but everything was wrong looking back.

✻ ✻ ✻

I can be changed by what happens to me.
But I refuse to be reduced by it.

—Maya Angelou

After I dropped my son off at school, my brother and I made the two-and-a-half-hour drive to Miami University to tell my oldest son, Kevin. On the way down, I contacted the college and explained why I was coming. They put me in touch with the RA in his dorm, who assured me that he was still sleeping and that his next class wasn't until 11:30.

We arrived at his dorm, but he didn't answer. When we went in, we found a bed piled high with bedding that seemed like he had been sleeping (literally a Ferris Bueller moment); however, he had probably slept at his fraternity and was already headed to class. At any other time, this would have been hilarious.

Ultimately, we had to go to his classroom, which, in a Murphy's Law moment, had two door openings, but he was smack dab in the middle and couldn't see us. Finally, we had no choice but to call the professor out, who then dismissed Kevin.

I had to tell my son in the hallway of his freshman class building that his dad not only died, but he died by suicide. By far the most horrendous, heartbreaking thing I have ever had to do. No child should ever be told this, and to this day, I cry every time I think of this moment. Sadly, this would not be the only moment. We had to get home so I could get my son, Ryan.

Kevin returned home with us and waited at the house while I picked Ryan up. While I told Kevin the truth of Chuck's death immediately, I wasn't ready to tell Ryan it was suicide until I had gotten counseling on how best to tell him.

I'm sure Ryan could sense something was wrong as we drove home, but I waited until we were inside to tell him that his dad had died of a heart attack. While the story could have been true, Ryan, being the logical boy that he is, said, "That's impossible. Dad does the 200-mile Pelotonia."

As parents, we make split-second decisions in times of acute trauma, and my decision to get Kevin first was one of my best. When Ryan was told, he ran into Kevin's arms, and I was so grateful they could support each other.

The second-best decision of this day was reaching out for support from our church youth group. This seems elementary; however, up to this point, I had never asked for help from anyone. This was a monumental shift in my own emotional growth, something that has been a huge part of my own personal transformation.

※ ※ ※

It is in times of great trauma when everything else is gone, knowing the Truth that we are never alone becomes part of survival.

In times of great emotional stress, we feel the most alone, and what I have learned is that we aren't. We just have to be patient and allow ourselves to be uncomfortable, and see the gifts we're being offered. The day of my husband's death, I had many.

At my lowest point, I had to reach out for help, and it changed the trajectory of my life. Until this point, my limiting beliefs convinced me I had no needs, that I could give to everyone and expect nothing in return. That I could handle anything; I was a rock for myself and everyone else.

My husband's suicide shattered everything in my carefully constructed life. That night, the youth group showed up, and my boys and their wonderful leaders sat around my kitchen table piled high with every dessert imaginable. They looked after my kids while I managed the steady stream of people who came to console us.

At some point, there was a lull. I remember looking out into the kitchen from the living room and wondering how my children would ever grow up whole, if they would get through this eventually. Then, out of the blue, someone told a joke. In the middle of the worst day imaginable, my kids, along with everyone else, were laughing hysterically. A gift from the Universe to tell me they would be OK one day.

Tears of joy and gratitude streamed from my face, and it was then that I had my own personal epiphany. A booming voice in my head stated succinctly, a voice I would later hear again during a meditation, "You are never going back to the way things were."

I didn't know why this was true, but I fully believed the words. Despite losing the one person who I felt provided my safety, albeit dysfunctionally, knowing I was more alone than I had ever been, I felt more connected to the rest of the world and something much larger than myself than I had ever felt before.

I realized I had been living with walls to protect myself, and although they did, they also prevented me from fully connecting with others. I used my willingness to give and feel needed as a false connection, rather than an authentic one. This revelation occurred to me that night, and I vowed never to put walls up again. I haven't.

I do not believe my experiences were unique to me. We each have these growth opportunities if we allow ourselves to be open to them. Figuratively, I had the cover ripped off me, and I feel truly blessed that I didn't revert to my normal homeostasis, but instead allowed myself to experience a different path.

The Universe, your Higher Power, God never leaves us; it's just sometimes we have to reach for help. I reached out, and it changed my life. We all have this potential opportunity; we just have to see it, and it often arises when we are being emotionally challenged and at our lowest.

My husband's death marked the end of who I was and the beginning of who I was supposed to be; essentially, my death and rebirth. My life was for everyone else, and I wrapped my self-worth up in people needing me, including my marriage. I was in a finance career I chose for practical reasons, and when I partnered with my husband in a financial services business he loved, I found no way out, even though I truly disliked the field.

Over the previous five years, I had been moving towards emotional growth, but the dynamics of my marriage made significant progress impossible. I was desperate for more authentic human connections, but couldn't create any when I wasn't being authentic with myself.

I was no longer the same person from the minute I heard about my husband's death. Everything I ever knew to be true and solid was gone. It was as if my internal hard drive had crashed, and I couldn't recover it. By the grace of God, I was in shock the first couple of weeks, so I could manage this incredibly emotionally stressful place.

One of nature's miracles is shock. For two weeks, I was literally alive but on autopilot at ten percent. Eating was impossible, drinking was a minimum, and every decision that had to be made was as if it was being made with me looking from afar.

The first night my kids were told, we decided to sleep in my king-size bed, which we had done many nights over the years for family movie night. It was my boy's idea, and I was again grateful I could be there for them as I had been throughout their lives.

At one point, Ryan had fallen asleep, and Kevin was having a very real unloading of all the things his dad would miss—his graduation, marriage, first child—then he was crying over the fact that the first thing his new fraternity brothers would know about him was that his dad took his life. I sobbed right along with him, and as I write this, the pain and loss are still there.

Sadly, Ryan was not asleep as we had thought, and this is how he found out his dad had taken his life. His blood-curdling scream will never leave me, and though it wasn't how I wanted him to find out, I had decided earlier that evening that we would not allow this to be our shame and that we would approach this honestly and head-on.

Ryan, always the logical one, finally stopped screaming and spoke seven words: "That was so ignorant of a choice." His words summarized it all.

Many people saved our lives that first week. Our church, First Community Church, stepped up in such an incredible way, providing emotional and physical support we could never have handled on our own. The youth group rallied around my kids and me, and the senior staff helped walk us through the service for my husband and arranged the after-service get-together.

I really just needed to decide the details as they asked, but mostly didn't have to do anything further. Friends helped us through the nightmare by being present, listening, and bringing meals. It was a time of significant loss and huge blessings; I didn't miss the contrast as it was happening.

The service took place on the Saturday after Chuck's death, and I will say I was completely unprepared for the number of people who showed up. There were other tremendous gifts for which I will forever be grateful. We had one calling hour period, just before the service, so we could minimize the emotional toll on the boys.

Still, I never expected the emotional stress this took. The receiving lines were miles long, wrapped around the streets of Grandview. This made me feel so good for my kids and so sad that Chuck never knew how much family and friends loved him. This was an emotionally strenuous two hours but so valuable. Halfway through, something happened that I will never forget as long as I live, and it literally changed Kevin's life view forever.

✺ ✺ ✺

Never underestimate the power of Love, support, and acceptance; sometimes, this is the difference between someone healing or not.

This weekend at Kevin's college was parents' weekend, which was even more important for kids like Kevin who were still freshmen. Kevin had chosen a fraternity by this point, and, based on the conversation we had in bed, I knew he was wondering if his fraternity brothers would accept him; he didn't have to wait long.

As the church receiving line rounded the corner, not less than 50 young men from Kevin's fraternity, all dressed in khakis and blue blazers, stood in line to offer their condolences. It was one of the most touching moments of my life, and their willingness to leave their own parents in Miami, driving the two and a half hours to support Kevin, was one of life's most beautiful memories and blessings for us.

These wonderful, compassionate young men floored me, many of whom might have never even attended a funeral before, never mind one where the person died by suicide. They saved Kevin in a million different ways that day. They saved all of us.

Both boys were insistent on participating in the service, so we tailored the service to meet their needs. Kevin delivered an amazingly honest, powerful, touching, and heartfelt tribute to his dad. I was in the front, and I was later told that everyone in the church was crying, including the fraternity boys from Miami. Kevin expressed himself with honesty and pain, and I know this was a huge milestone in his healing.

Ryan was to perform in a viola competition the morning of Chuck's funeral, so he opted to play the song he had practiced as a tribute to his dad. For as long as I live, I'll remember Ryan walking from his seat to the altar in his adorable Calvin Klein black suit, which he would never wear again, and with so much poise, telling everyone that what he was about to play was in honor of his dad. Again, not a dry eye in the place as Ryan delivered the song perfectly, a song that he and the pianist had never practiced. We are never alone, and wonderful gifts happen if we let them. I have never been prouder of my two boys and never sadder for their loss.

We all went back to my home after the service, and over two hundred people came with us, including all the fraternity boys. The church had arranged an incredible amount of food, and despite it being February, the warm 58-degree day drew people inside, outside, and downstairs. Although it was such an overwhelmingly sad day, we were surrounded by so much Love, and it didn't escape me that this was just the beginning of our journey as a family. I felt hopeful that we would get through whatever was necessary.

Kevin decided a few days after the funeral that he wanted to go back to college, and though I was reluctant to send him, he promised to continue therapy for a year, which helped assuage my fears. I also had a conversation with both boys before he left, and I reiterated that their father's death wasn't and will never be our shame and that I will never allow them to use his death as an excuse; life lessons that I learned as a child.

Growth was coming rapidly for me, and I realized I had enabled my husband for 21 years, just as his mother had. I realized that his learned helplessness and lack of resiliency had caused what transpired, even though he was a brilliant man. I vowed to stop the behavior with my boys after seeing the damage firsthand.

So many people helped us in the early days, from Ryan's elementary school staff coming to the house to support us to his middle school counselor coming to the house to ask how she could help make his transition back to school easier, to a friend who was a social worker who could line my kids up with counseling the first week.

The wheels of life turned while I was on hold, and somehow life went on. Ryan eventually went back to school as well, and upon his return, his guidance counselor organized a private lunch in her office with six of his best friends.

So many people stepped up, and I let them. That's the truly amazing part.

Chapter 2

We don't heal in isolation; we heal in community.

—Joyce Meyer

✹

THE HARDEST PART of a traumatic event is the initial shock, but once the shock starts wearing off, that's when the real work begins. Kevin and Ryan were both back at school, and now I had the arduous task of figuring out who I was, what to do with the business Chuck and I shared, and how to create a new life.

The first step was the business since we were managing people's money, and time was of the essence. I probably could have sold the business for money, but emotionally, my only aim was to save the clients (always looking out for everyone else) and take the pressure off myself.

Going back to the office was impossible, and to this day, I have never set foot in the building. I think it's human nature to discount the trauma of something and its lasting impact, preferring to bury it instead. After all, there's only so much we can take.

I saw this firsthand approximately a year after Chuck's death. Our sales assistant had hit a huge milestone in passing the securities exam, and I knew Chuck would have wanted to give her a gift, so I met her outside the building where he had died. I was only there for a few minutes before I had a panic attack, and I realized I had not processed this piece at all—so many layers of traumatic loss.

I, too, started seeing a therapist and found my savior, though he was very unorthodox by most people's standards. My first and most prominent emotion initially was the overwhelming guilt I felt for my husband's death. I felt as though I was carrying 100-pound weights on each shoulder with every step.

This therapist was one of the best, though very much tough love, which I was all for since I wanted the fast track to digging in deep. I did not know my journey would take years just to heal all my baggage, including the suicide and my childhood; it's probably just as well I was clueless. This therapist was both harsh and caring, and the first day I will never forget.

I expressed the guilt I felt, and he literally screamed at me, "You are (expletive) delusional if you think you caused your husband's death, and if you stick with me for at least six months, you'll agree." I wasn't sure about his style, but I was sure of the need to believe him, and so I embarked on my journey with this tough love therapist.

In between therapy sessions the first year, I did what I always have done best, and that was to keep busy. The strategy wasn't horrible, though it was a defensive measure. I realized much later that it needed to change. I'm sure people thought I was tough as nails, organizing a parenting group in the first few months that met every month during the first year, getting involved in flipping houses with a friend, and still managing to hold down the fort at home.

I soon started running again, which had always been my stress relief since childhood, and more or less, life went on.

In my marriage, I had done virtually everything related to the house and kids, and it was very noticeable how much I did after Chuck died. We didn't skip a beat.

A year later, I became a suicide grief facilitator, and one of the hardest parts of grief is trying to manage life while you are grieving. This was not a problem for me at all. Sad statement on my marriage, but I was grateful I had the luxury of grieving at my own pace.

True to my goal, I kept no more walls. I started reaching out for help when I needed it, and though it still feels uncomfortable today, I know it's important to let others help me as I help them. It has taken me much longer to realize that giving is not part of my self-worth.

What's interesting is how our outward persona becomes so entrenched that everyone, including ourselves, starts to believe the narrative. To me and everyone else in my world, I was a Type A, assertive, hard-charging, giving, never-say-no, caring person, there for everyone. I had high self-esteem, and I ran my life.

Turns out this wasn't entirely true.

As my therapy progressed, I knew I needed a new therapist who was more versed in childhood issues, finally recognizing that my problems started way before my marriage and husband's death, and, in fact, every decision had resulted from my childhood beliefs. So, we parted ways, and I began the next part of my journey with an amazing therapist who began tackling my childhood traumas.

✱ ✱ ✱

We can try to run faster than our childhood programming and trauma, but eventually, the traumas will always catch up with us.

Spiritually, things started changing dramatically. Virtually everything that I once knew and relied on seemed to vanish. This was a period of acute emotional disorganization, and it was a very challenging time for me personally. I started having more vivid dreams about myself and emotional views, and what is even more startling is that people who had recently experienced a loved one's suicide started reaching out to me randomly.

Without realizing it, I had begun "companioning" people, a term used by a volunteer group—LOSS: Local Outreach to Suicide Survivors—that I later joined and became an active volunteer. Looking back, I was open to everything, as painful as it was, and Divine Intercession was all around me.

Helping others heal became a cathartic healing process for me as well. Soon, I became an actual "companion" for survivors, also volunteering as a grief support group facilitator. In helping others, I was helping myself.

At this point in my journey, I was getting a better sense of what my trauma and programming were, both from childhood and my husband's death, yet surprises happened often. While I was becoming much more conscious, I was also having to face my deepest wounds, many of which were based on a false narrative I had told myself and deeply believed about myself and my childhood family.

One day, I was at my new therapist's office, and I was in a sad place about my relationship with Chuck. Though I had successfully fought off the great demon, guilt, there was still a layer of feeling like I had failed Chuck by not recognizing the demons he was fighting. I recall my therapist asking if I would try an exercise to help me, and I agreed.

We both got up in a football stance, facing one another, hands touching and extending outwards, and I had to push him across the room while he resisted, and I had to say repeatedly, "I failed you." It was exceedingly emotional, and I cried deeply.

Next, I was to do the same exercise; however, this time, I was to say, "Chuck failed me." For ten minutes, I could not utter those words, words that applied to many people in my past, words and feelings that I never acknowledged.

I finally relented, did the exercise, and cried deeper than I ever had. Upon ending the exercise, I was asked to express how I felt without thought. My answer shocked me, "worthless," I whispered. This began my true healing.

I have always been a resilient, confident person, and, from anyone's opinion, I had high self-esteem and practiced unconditional self-love. This is what I thought as well; this was also completely untrue. After years of "getting past" my childhood trauma and creating a substantial life, I realized the damage was far deeper, and it really highlighted the fact that our deepest fears and limiting beliefs are so deep that seeing them is often very challenging.

I also learned that uncovering this is the key to rewriting our childhood story and was the best chance for internal peace, unconditional love towards oneself, and true healing. I believe we all have these stories that need to be uncovered. My therapist retired later that winter, and I will be forever grateful for the springboard he afforded me that day toward my growth and consciousness.

After discovering how much I had hidden from myself, I began to see the patterns in my life's journey. While I had historically seen strength and resilience, I realized that this strength and resilience also helped construct walls that kept me from my truest self, and worse, deep connections with others that I longed for. I also started to see the lack of boundaries in my life, though I still had many lessons to learn before I finally grasped it.

While I logically understood what was lacking in my wholeness, I still didn't recognize how it played out in every facet of my life, but most noticeably in romantic relationships and other close friendships. Programming made me feel guilty about my successes, even though I had worked hard for them, convincing myself that I was fortunate to have more resilience and fortitude than most others.

Because of my giving nature, I felt compelled to share my rewards with others. I now know that this was just my ego, preventing me from seeing the deep pain and guilt I had inside, but back then, you couldn't have convinced me of that. I wasn't yet ready.

Throughout my life, I felt overly responsible for those I loved and freely gave my time, emotional support, and money. I felt it was necessary to help my family, friends, and even relative strangers, often feeling like I was a "good" person, versus the worthless person I was hiding from myself. I was codependent in every sense and had very few boundaries.

We planned very well for the future, so when my husband died, along with the insurance proceeds, I could live comfortably while I was healing and helping my boys to do the same. There is so much gratitude for Chuck taking care of us in the manner he did. The week before he died, he uncharacteristically tidied everything up so the transition from two parents to one was about as smooth as it could be.

I felt tremendous guilt about my financial position, even though it was largely a result of decades of planning and saving. Because of this, I gave freely. Within two months of my husband's death, a friend who was struggling financially asked me to help her restore and flip houses.

This was an idea we had previously tossed around, so it didn't occur to me that I was emotionally unprepared for the extra stress that being 100 percent financially liable would put on me. I saw it as a great service to my friend and ended up flipping three houses.

In retrospect, none of these properties were in my best interest and, in fact, increased my stress due to the financial risk. The portion I took from the sale did not at all justify the risk whatsoever; I could have made much more elsewhere with much less stress. I didn't see this at all.

I wrapped myself up in giving to escape the feelings of entitlement, guilt, and emptiness, and helping in any way seemed okay, but in truth, it made no sense. Do I regret helping my friend? Absolutely not, but I wouldn't do it again under the same circumstances.

When I finally started healing, the cloud lifted, and I started seeing things much differently than I had. Every choice we make, every friendship or relationship we have, will be influenced by unconscious wounds and beliefs about ourselves until we discover and heal them.

Chapter 3

*The Universe is relentless in giving
us opportunities to grow.*

❋

APPROXIMATELY SEVENTEEN MONTHS after Chuck's death, I was out running one night, and I received a frantic call from a girlfriend's husband asking if I could reach out to his wife after she had just learned a close friend of hers had taken her life. We spoke for a couple of hours, and I willingly offered her my love and support, aware of the journey both she and her friend's family and loved ones would embark on.

Once you have gone through your own hell and tragedy, to me, it is impossible to look away from someone else's similar experience. Grieving is a nonlinear process with ebbs and flows, and I knew all too well what my friend would deal with. I also offered support to her friend's family for the same reasons.

My friend and I spoke daily, and within three weeks, she felt concerned that her friend's husband was not managing well and asked if I would offer support. Naturally, I said yes.

I reached out, and we made plans to meet a couple of days after July 4th that year. This soon became another life-altering experience.

Toxic relationships don't always become apparent from the start. Though in retrospect, there were red flags everywhere, it was my own neediness that prevented me from seeing them—a neediness I had buried my entire life. Within a short period, after having spoken for three hours the first day, we became romantically involved.

I can tell you all the red flags that were present. However, this story isn't about the other party and what he did wrong, which was plenty. The actual story is about what toxic relationships help us see about ourselves.

From literally the first day, I was told wonderful things about myself that I had never heard before—I was the most beautiful, smartest, insightful, caring, and sexy person who walked the planet. I was so emotionally wounded and had such a deep longing to be seen and loved. I wanted to believe these things were all true, even though this man didn't actually know me yet.

Time progressed rapidly from "we just met each other" to "we need to get married." Everything was on an accelerated path to close the deal as quickly as possible. Within a month of our first meeting, cracks began to appear. Still, even though the cracks were enormous, I refused to acknowledge them, instead accepting the false apologies for him, once again telling me how wonderful I was.

Within three months, his true colors came out in a myriad of ways. Though I knew this wasn't love, I was so addicted to his apologies and affirmations, often multiple times a week, that I started believing this was the real deal, even though I intuitively knew I should run. This person was not kind, though he often made a show of kindness by buying concert tickets, fancy dinners, and even offering to purchase me a Lexus on my first birthday with him. I declined.

This man, I believe, wanted to be with me, although I now know for every wrong reason possible, mainly to "win," as he put it. I was a challenge—the girl he couldn't overpower or control with his charisma and money; the combination to my heart he never understood.

After six months in the relationship, I spent another year attempting to emotionally and physically disengage myself from him. We ended things at least a dozen times, only for me to be lured back in with false promises of change and growth. Often, I reached out, missing the validation he gave me.

Each lie he told, each time he was verbally abusive, each time his values contradicted mine, each time his mask of perfection came off, each time he projected his unwanted traits and actions onto me, I knew the relationship had to end. My attachment to something that was entirely unhealthy for me and, truthfully, for him as well was what I later found to be a trauma bond, a leftover from childhood programming.

Sometimes we can fall in love with the very person who is destroying us, yet is giving us the opportunity to heal at the same time. What we don't acknowledge about ourselves will undoubtedly repeat as experiences until we take notice. Early on, it became apparent this person had addiction issues, and within a year after many interventions, I was driving three hours away to take him to inpatient rehab for three weeks.

Though I was hopeful, I had seen his empty promises so many times, and his ability to use his charisma to work the system. I was not overly optimistic. Initially, it appeared he was taking things seriously, often preaching for hours by phone about what he had learned. Despite all the things he had done to me, forgiveness was easy—a skill I had mastered as a small child. Forgiving damage to my children, however, was harder.

A week before the rehab, which was a "lose your job or go to rehab" scenario, this person had said something so egregious and despicable to my son that it needed to be addressed. I had tried previously, and he attempted to apologize, but he essentially swept it under the rug and left me longing for closure.

During the rehab, I brought the situation up, and instead of handling it with the growth that he insisted he had achieved in the intense preceding two weeks of treatment, he went nuts and screamed and verbally abused me, so much so that I hung up.

He was clearly playing his game, which he had learned from his childhood. I now knew the relationship was hopeless and really tried at this point to separate. Still crazy in love with him, leaving was a challenge. Looking back, though, I realized I was only in love with the way he made me feel. I knew this from my head. My heart had a different perspective.

For the next several months, I tried everything in my power to align my heart with my head, with varying degrees of success on different days. During this time, I also focused on healing the wounds that were still raw, so that such a relationship would never happen again.

Within a month, three months with minimal contact, I met a man who made me overjoyed. I had recently completed a 26-week certification in life coaching and was ready to embark on a new spiritual path. I met this new man, and it was shocking how closely our histories aligned.

We both come from dysfunctional families with an absentee father, whom we never knew, and a stepfather who was emotionally damaging. We were both star athletes in high school and college, which afforded us a ticket out of our childhood drama. Both of us worked in financial services for 25 years, then left for something more fulfilling. We both had marriages that ended, his by divorce, but not too dissimilar to mine in context. We both had two kids we adored, we both believed in a Higher Power, and lastly, he had a Leadership Coaching business that mirrored mine.

In literally every facet, we matched up. Quickly, I fell in love and was happy to put the other relationship behind me. The problem was that this new man was telling a story, and it had no resemblance to the life he was actually living.

It soon became obvious that actions and words did not match up if I had only cared to notice early on. In virtually every category, it turns out that the story was beautiful, but the reality was not so much.

He was an absentee dad, he did not have a business instead working for a company delivering "canned" presentations, though he was quite skilled, the circumstances of his divorce were fabricated and embellished, he lied about where he lived, he had a drinking problem by my definition, and again, all these things were clear from day one, had I chosen to notice.

I was so enamored with the story that I overlooked the actions in favor of believing the fantasy. I fell deeply in love, and once again, I was in a toxic relationship. Now, in fairness, the second relationship was much less toxic than the first. By the time we met, I had done a considerable amount of healing, and I was meeting my own needs much more substantially. I fell in love with who I thought he was, and the letdown was considerable.

Almost like clockwork, three months arrived. He did something particularly egregious and literally broke my heart. I challenged him, and we stayed together off and on for more time, but by now, his mask was off, and his wounds prevented him from connecting to me in any meaningful way.

Now, I realized I was attracting the same person on an emotional level, fooled because the human level seemed so different. Falling in love with someone's mask is never pleasant. As my Spirit Guides told me, "He is nothing more than another pop quiz from the Universe." It took me a while to accept this.

Again, my heart needed to catch up with my head, and I spent many months hoping the man I had fallen in love with would come back. Unlike the first man, who I felt was so oblivious, at least to me, the second, I believed (and still do), was fully capable of significant growth and change but lacked the willingness to achieve it.

Growing up in a family where love was non-existent, I grew up with a longing for a deep attachment, gave 100 percent of myself to my relationships to the best of my ability, and felt that by doing so, others would reciprocate. It could be, but not with the wrong person. Both broke my heart, and in doing so, they helped me grow and heal.

✺ ✺ ✺

The key to emotional and spiritual growth is willingness. Without it, nothing can or will change.

After the first relationship, I knew I had my own issues to work on, and on a good day, I felt gratitude for having them exposed so callously. On a bad day, I felt hurt and resentful that I had been so poorly treated. In hindsight, I assumed I had healed after man one, but this was not even close to the case. Lesson learned: One can't heal if they don't actually know the problem, and lesson two, as Albert Einstein said, "No problem can be solved from the *same* level of *consciousness* that *created* it." I didn't fully understand this, but on some level, I felt it.

I would like to say that, after all the above, which is truly a snippet of what took place (this is my story, not theirs), I experienced tremendous healing and moved on to greener pastures full of joy, peace, and self-love. This, of course, is not how life works.

Becoming more conscious and healing is as fast as you want to make it, but it is hard work, discipline, and most importantly, a willingness to want to change. Willingness is truly everything because without this one quality, unconscious defenses and one's own ego will stay firmly fixed in the past and will dictate the future.

I was such a giver, altruistic to fault, kind, and deeply empathic. I never believed I was being ruled by ego. This turned out to be far from the truth. For most of us who are being ruled by our subconscious, by definition, we have to be ruled by our lower self or ego, since our higher self is covered with layers of limiting beliefs and false ideas about who we are.

Not that I am not innately altruistic, kind, giving, and deeply empathic. I have these traits. The distinguishing fact is what my intentions were behind these actions. This simple knowledge was the gift of two consecutive toxic relationships. Both parties have to be complicit or vibrations and energies wouldn't align, and there wouldn't even be a relationship because we would be out of sync.

If we aligned, it was easy to see that I must have played a part as well. I desperately wanted to know what that part was because I never wanted to attract a similar partner again. It turns out that like attracts like in terms of vibration. So, if I were just as complicit, what was my role in both these relationships, even my marriage, and every relationship I had ever had?

This was the turning point in my growth and increasing consciousness, and was also the point where I could only see gratitude for all the people in my life, and most recently in the two relationships and marriage. Before, I saw hurt and resentment, or even understanding, which was a foil for a lack of true understanding.

I now knew that things weren't personal as I had often felt. These men and even my parents were just being themselves. I just put myself in the firing line. In my pre-birth plan, I chose my parents so they could set the stage for the relationship and attachments I would seek, and I did just that. I found the exact emotional replicas of both my parents, and by doing so, took off scabs that took a lifetime to create.

In the end, they were living out their own emotional trauma. We were equally dysfunctional and equally damaging to one another. This was a hard pill to swallow, though it was an absolute truth and necessary for me to face at the deepest levels.

I never saw myself as needy. After all, I have been taking care of most people for most of my life. I am incredibly resilient. Nothing knocks me down. Even after Chuck's suicide, I knew I would survive.

Yet, even though all of this is true, what I didn't realize was that my incredible resilience and strength did not allow for needs or any vulnerability whatsoever; without vulnerability, we can't authentically connect to others. This dynamic shaped my marriage. We both had deep wounds and walls, and neither pushed the other to knock them down.

It wasn't until 15 years into my marriage that I felt an urge for more, and the boat became unbalanced. This would have been fine if both people rowing continued rowing at the same pace, but this was not my marriage. I was rowing faster, and Chuck was rowing at the same speed he had always rowed, and this was not a good recipe for staying metaphorically afloat.

The few times I cried in my marriage, I recall my husband's reaction rather than the bemusement I thought I saw. I now see fear in the potential unraveling of our marriage. Had he lived, it's hard to say where we would be. My Soul was yearning for more, desperate to get out of the prison I had created.

Chapter 4

The Universe doesn't like denial; it will keep sending you opportunities to see the Truth and awaken.

✷

THESE "MELTDOWNS" WERE actually nudges from the universe, nudges that we all get if we care to notice. I was so defended against vulnerability of any kind that I was completely unaware of the message I was being sent.

After the ending of both relationships and the awareness of my part, even if I initially hadn't had a clue what my part was, I started paying more attention. After Chuck died, within a month, I began a desperate search for a spiritual advisor, having lost the one I had when she died five years prior.

I began an exhaustive search online, and each time I did, I came up with the same person, Rosalie Strawcutter, despite changing the search criteria. After a while, I realized this, too, was a nudge from the Universe, a nudge that would send my life on a much-needed course correction.

I had my first spiritual reading with Rosalie in April, two months after Chuck died. I had the reading over the phone,

The Stories We Tell Ourselves 193

preferring to keep some distance in case the fit wasn't good. Within minutes of speaking with Rosalie, I felt a kinship that I couldn't explain and wouldn't understand until a few years later.

During our first call, Rosalie explained the details of my husband's death, the emotional state he was in when he took his life, described my boys and how their life had unfolded, and what it would look like in the future, and even channeled my parents, who divulged things that no one knew but me. I had found the right person to help me on my journey.

Before long, I was spending an hour a month with Rosalie, "speaking" with my husband to find answers to the unimaginable.

Unlike natural deaths, suicides don't afford one the ability to claim "God's Will," romanticize the relationship, heal, or move on. Suicide, from my worldview, is never God's Will, although I realize it is definitely an option in some people's life plan. Through countless hours of mediumship readings, channeling loved ones, spirit guide contact, and Akashic Records, it is my belief that not only do we choose our parents, but we also choose our death, or what the astral plane calls death, exit points. Each Soul has points in their life to choose to exit, and, in fact, many of us, if we think back, are aware of times when there could have been an exit. I have had several; two that stand out.

The first was in college. After a sleepless weekend in DC, I had the chore to drive back from Long Island, NY, to CT. I was exhausted and should have admitted this, but in true form, not wanting to let anyone down, I agreed to drive while everyone else fell asleep.

I was literally doing everything in my power to keep my eyes open, and then when I woke up, the car was on the side of the road with the engine still running on the Long Island Expressway, cars speeding by. I have no recollection of pulling over, parking, or falling asleep while driving, yet I arrived safely on the side of the road.

The second involved my husband and me when we traveled to San Francisco for our honeymoon. We had a highly sought-after restaurant reservation at Wolfgang Puck, but our flight was late, and we were growing impatient. There were way more passengers than taxis, and it became very apparent we might miss our reservation when, out of the blue, a driver appeared to offer us a ride. He had a taxi sign, and though it wasn't a taxi, which seemed odd (this was long before Uber or Lyft), we grabbed the chance to make our reservation.

Chuck got in the front, and by the time the driver was pulling away, I knew something felt off. I tried to get Chuck's attention, but I wasn't sure what I was going to do; he was engaged in a conversation with the driver. As the distance from the airport got longer, my intuition got louder, and I knew something was wrong, even if I couldn't place what it was.

Within a minute of this last thought, the car started sputtering, and the next thing we knew, the driver pulled over and bolted into the woods next to the highway. We were speechless until, within minutes, a police officer came out of nowhere and stopped. After chastising us for getting in, he informed us it was a stolen vehicle, and we were most likely going to be robbed, stranded, or worse. He told us how blessed we were that the driver ran out of gas.

Both times, I believe, were exit points, and each time, our own guardian angels miraculously saved us. The timing wasn't right; we had more work to do here on a Soul level. Looking back from the spiritual vantage point where I currently am, I see these as opportunities to see the hand of the Divine at play. They were potential exit points and also potential opportunities to reevaluate our lives, understand the magnitude of what had taken place, and take the opportunity for spiritual growth.

Neither of these two exit points and outcomes could have happened by coincidence; our Souls needed more time. Two months before Chuck died, Chuck was bringing leaves to the dump in our 14-year-old Cadillac Escalade and lost the brakes on a busy highway going downhill at 35 miles per hour through the intersection. Somehow, as he described that day, the cars, which were always steady at a speed of 50 miles per hour, parted, and he made it through to a park unscathed. This was an incredible anomaly and made zero sense. When he called to get a ride, I recall I felt no shock. It was more like, "Of course he is okay," though this was a very odd reaction.

A few years later, during a reading with Rosalie, I asked about this, only recently remembering that he had lost his brakes only two months previous to his suicide, wondering why that wasn't his exit point, which would have saved some of the trauma for the kids.

His answer was interesting. Chuck acknowledged that losing the brakes on the Escalade was indeed an exit point. However, if it had happened, many, many other people would have been affected, and the outcome for me and my boys would have been extremely messy with lawsuits galore. He said that his suicide was indeed another chosen exit point and that if he was supposed to have lived, he would have, and in fact, this wasn't the only time in his life he had considered this. The others were thwarted.

While it's still difficult for me to rationalize suicide from a human perspective, from a Soul's perspective, it makes more sense. Chuck further explained that exit points are in consideration of everyone's highest and best good for each Soul involved, and a car death wouldn't have accomplished that. He said his suicide was necessary to facilitate quicker financial closure so I could be emotionally present for the boys and that the suicide could also be beneficial for his father, with whom he had a complicated relationship, regardless of whether he learned from it.

The Divine provides the opportunity, while choice and willingness determine if the door stays open or shuts. Many years later, I had complete closure on the suicide during an afterlife reading with Laura Scott. Laura's gifts lie in accessing the past through conversations with Ascended Masters, seeing a record of every thought, emotion, or action ever taken, felt, or experienced by every Soul, and she could look into the past lives I had with Chuck.

I knew we had a spiritual connection from the first day, even if we didn't acknowledge it. From the first word, there was complete comfort and familiarity that went way past our complimentary wounding, which also factored in. Laura's reading this day changed my perspective and changed the story I had been telling about my husband's death and our marriage.

During this reading, I was speaking with Laura about exit points and how this possibly correlated with past lives. She had previously mentioned that in that life, Chuck and I had known one another in the fourteenth century and that we were brother and sister. I was the stable one in that lifetime but still looked up to my brother, refusing to see the truth about his opium addiction.

Chuck eventually died a natural death, though he was weeks away from dying because of his addiction. As his sister, I never recovered. Instead, I fell into a deep depression, refusing to accept the truth of my brother, eventually being killed by a horse as I darted erratically through the street, lost in my grief.

This story is plausible, especially for the family emotions I carried from the first day I met Chuck in this lifetime. On this day, Laura described another lifetime. In this incarnation, Chuck was a wealthy landowner. I was a very happy, free-spirited woman, and we had two boys, the same two boys

I have today. Chuck died of sepsis since this was before antibiotics, and I tried picking up the financial pieces.

As a wealthy property owner, my husband collected taxes each month, and we lived a very comfortable life. After he died, I had no authority as a woman, so I had to hire a collector to help with the collections. Initially, the man took ten percent, but as time went on, he kept taking more until my boys and I were getting nothing. Women had no rights, so no one cared, and before long, we were homeless and separated to live as best we could. I ended up as a housekeeper for a family. The boys went their own way, and we never had the family together again. All of us died lonely deaths at a young age. Laura explained that this death was to undo that karma. In this lifetime, Chuck made sure we were financially safe when he left, so I could devote my energy, without worry, to raising my boys.

Through Laura, he said, "It was the best moment of my life; my finest achievement this lifetime." What's so amazing is how resentful I was when he died, leaving me with the mess of trying to raise my boys without long-term emotional damage, and yet he made sure I would do just that; truly his finest achievement. I'm so grateful.

Chapter 5

*When trauma becomes obsessive,
it's because closure is elusive.*

※

FOR THE FIRST year after Chuck's suicide, I read every book I could get my hands on relative to suicide, psychology, and relationships, well over a hundred books, trying to make sense of the senseless. I remember having obsessive thoughts 24/7 about Chuck that were literally driving me crazy. I would go to bed praying to be released from my compulsive thoughts so that I could actually sleep. The "loop," as it is called in grief support groups, while normal, is extremely debilitating. It's very hard to focus on anything else when your head can only replay the same reel over and over.

This went on for an entire year. One day, almost a year to the day, I was driving through town, while begging for Chuck to help me understand why he took his life, mostly unconsciously seeking freedom from my guilt.

By now, I had had many unnatural occurrences in my house—lights blinking on and off; garage door not working, then working; a can of soda sliding six inches on a countertop dry as a bone underneath; my dog, Lilly, acting uncharacteristically hyper, running in circles and "smiling" towards the sky; so I knew Chuck was around most days.

On this day, I was begging him to please release me from my torment when suddenly, while driving, I saw a billboard flash within my mind so quickly I thought I was imagining it. As I turned the corner, the billboard came again, this time very slowly, and it stated in bold letters, "disconnected."

I pulled over, recognizing that this was Chuck explaining in one word how he felt, disconnected, which made all the sense in the world why he took his life, and the billboard was actually a stock market ticker tape, so appropriate to let me know who was sending my message.

Fast forward a year, and I met a 71-year-old minister who asked if I was married. I told him my story and mentioned the disconnected sign. When I did, he started sobbing. He explained to me that 35 years earlier, he had attempted suicide, and he could tell no one because he could not find the words to explain how he felt during that period in his life. He said "disconnected" was exactly how he felt. We both healed a little more that evening, grateful for the nudge from the Universe. We meet exactly who we are supposed to meet at exactly the right time, for everyone's highest and best good.

Once I understood where Chuck was emotionally, I was no longer obsessed with trying to understand. It was still heartbreaking; however, I could now let go of guilt and replace it with regret, which is monumentally different and essential to healing.

From this point on, my spiritual world changed. I had been a seeker of my Higher Power since childhood and attended churches regularly throughout my adult life, even at this point, acting as a youth leader and sitting on various church councils. Though I sought anchoring in something more than myself, I was still seeking more than formal religion. My attention focused on ancient spiritual teachings, the afterlife, soul contracts, karma, and much more.

There is a saying that when we are open, the right things will find us. This became the cornerstone of everything in my life.

✷ ✷ ✷

Grief has its own timeline; give it space to move as it needs to. Rushing it will only delay the healing.

Eventually, it became apparent that I needed to put my faith in something greater than myself and surrender to the uncomfortable feelings that go along with not knowing where one is going, trusting that the path will find itself.

I still worked hard. Life isn't about being a passive passenger, but I was slowly letting go of the need to make things happen. Early in my initial grieving, I vowed I would not rush the process. For once, I vowed to live authentically, fully believing, as Brene Brown said, "We cannot selectively numb emotions; when we numb the painful emotions, we also numb the positive emotions." As a result, I committed to feeling every emotion that crossed my path.

Mostly, I would have a feeling, and a book would arrive as a recommendation or randomly cross my path, such as *Braving the Wilderness* by Brené Brown. I would find exactly what I needed to help me on my healing journey. I would finish one book, which usually created more questions, and another would materialize. This happened repeatedly, and at some point, I knew I was being Divinely guided.

I continued to reach out to my church-based faith and spiritual helpers for help in my life direction. I rarely asked for mundane things from my spiritual advisors, choosing to focus on the bigger picture, intuitively knowing that the big picture would also fix the little picture.

For a long time, one of my biggest needs was Love. Back then, I felt an underlying anxiety at all times, something I didn't know I had until I didn't anymore, and I was often asking about future Love, erroneously believing Love is something you find versus something we are. Many times, I would be told by my late mother or late husband that I wasn't ready yet, that I needed to Love myself unconditionally first, so that I wouldn't be choosing from a place of lack. Initially, I just didn't understand what I was being told. After all, I was so confident, had high self-esteem, and asked for nothing. How could there be a lack?.

Much later, I realized my high self-esteem was ego-driven, along with my confidence and lack of needs, while my Higher Self was crying to be seen. Getting to the source of this was very difficult. It was also the very best thing that ever happened to me as an adult.

Around this time, I was really coming to terms with my marriage to Chuck and understanding what had actually taken place. I learned I loved him and still do, as true love never truly dissipates; however, the equal relationship I had longed for had morphed over the 21 years into more of a parent-child relationship, a relationship I thought was the essence of true love.

By the time I had met Chuck, I was in my thirties, as was he, and we were both deeply entrenched in our respective limiting beliefs. He was actually emotionally tough by nature but conditioned to learned helplessness.

I was innately very sensitive, but I was convinced that I was completely resilient with few emotional needs. I started branching out socially and started seeing marriages that were more equally aligned, pushing for more equality in my own. The idea that people need to grow together is not a cliche; it is a fundamental truth. While I was pushing for growth, Chuck was pushing for the status quo. Emotional intimacy was non-existent, though I never dreamed that Chuck was hiding his own demons.

* * *

> *The stories we tell ourselves can be so ingrained that we believe them to be the Truth. It's shocking to find out they were just fiction.*

Subconsciously, throughout my entire marriage, I felt I was "bad" and Chuck was "good." I cleaned up every mess, battled every conflict, and made all the hard choices while running our financial life, physical home, and the children's lives; subconsciously, this was to prove I was worthy. Every decision that was made rested on me, and Chuck had the luxury of being good cop 24/7. I believed in him fully and, from the very beginning, carried my unacknowledged shame into the relationship, allowing myself to buy into the fact that Chuck was of utmost integrity and emotionally unequipped.

I stoically handled every lawsuit, every tax audit, and every household problem while Chuck watched from the sidelines, often not even telling him, so I didn't have to subject him to the extra stress. He had indeed become another child in the home. Chuck might have accepted this role, but I allowed it.

There were many times throughout my life that I had breakthroughs, but since my ego was largely leading me, my growth was still rather limited. I knew I had baggage and even knew what was in the suitcase. Yet, I hadn't fully unpacked it, so I was still learning about its impact. The ego is a great protector, especially as children, when we are ill-equipped to handle the emotional chaos thrown at us. My ego saved me in childhood and inhibited me in adulthood. At some point, and I don't believe I'm unique, we become our ego. Even if it served us well at one point, in adulthood, it only serves to move us further away from our authentic self.

Slowly but surely, I was learning about myself and the falsehoods that I had learned and fully believed. My husband used to defer all conflict to me because, as he put it, "You don't mind it." This was always untrue, but I believed I didn't mind it, and more so, I didn't hide from it because adults do what is necessary.

What I have found out is that I actually abhor conflict. I will continue to do what is necessary; however, I am now in touch with how I really feel. What's interesting is that previously, when handling conflict, I would become almost aggressive, using force to accomplish what I needed to. Today, I am very calm in conflict, acting assertively, and instead of my force, I have replaced it with power. My energetic vibrations have risen as my consciousness has grown, and even though in the past my lower energy of shame had me use force to accomplish things, I now use power and complete things effortlessly with very little emotional energy or forethought.

I didn't understand the power of this concept until I came across a YouTube video of Dr. David Hawkins discussing his book, *Power vs. Force*, and it all made sense. Once again, the Universe delivered exactly what I needed when I was ready to hear it.

Since that first video, I have listened to dozens of his videos and even joined a study group that reads and delves into Dr. Hawkins's books, which focus on raising one's consciousness. A few years ago, his work would have never resonated with me.

One concept that Dr. Hawkins has developed is the "Scale of Consciousness," which explains that each of us enters a carnation with a level of consciousness and lives out the lessons from that level. The scale ranges from 0 to 1000, with avatars such as Jesus and Buddha at 1000, and the rest at lower levels.

The premise is that anyone who calibrates below 200 is taking from humanity and is living more from a survival perspective. Anyone above 200 is giving and adding to the positivity of humanity. What's noteworthy is that the calibration is the energy that is inside, not the mask that one shows the world.

This knowledge has affected me because I have been in relationships with people who present as one way, but their vibration or energy doesn't seem to agree. As I have become closer to my true self and more in touch with my own higher intuition, I can sense the difference, and most of the time, instantly.

I have often been told that we all have intuitive powers, and until the past couple of years of questioning this, I now know this to be true. We are all given the ability to see the Truth in others once we see the Truth in ourselves, and this becomes our genuine power. Ego defenses might help us get through childhood difficulties, and once served us well, but can often become a hindrance in adulthood. Once we know the Truth about ourselves, no matter what it is, we can't ever unsee it. This is the first step towards emotional wholeness, but it takes tremendous courage.

For most of us, our ego saved us, but also built a prison where escape is very challenging. It's hard to imagine waking up and realizing one's whole life has been false. We were only playing a character we invented based on the stories we told ourselves. We easily lie to others because we are lying to ourselves.

Knowing I felt worthless was one of the hardest things for me to accept. I was a superstar in every way. How could this be possible? But I knew it was my Truth. I knew I couldn't unsee it, couldn't put it back in the vault with the shame that caused it. The Truth was out, and now I had to face it. Most people, thankfully, will never have a trauma as bad as mine, where my metaphorical cover was ripped off the ball and the self I knew and had so carefully guarded was obliterated in one knock on my door.

As I mentioned previously, I was so dismantled that I figured I might as well see what was in the vault, since I really did not know who I was anymore. While many of us will blessedly not have anything so catastrophic, we all have our own version of trauma, and we all have huge nudges if we see them.

My trauma is huge, but any trauma is just as huge to the person experiencing it. Divorce, chronic illness, addiction, getting fired, kids leaving home, and more. Any of these can provide a psychological shattering, and how we choose to react to it is the key.

Chapter 6

Coincidences are God's way of remaining anonymous.

—**Albert Einstein**

✹

ONE OF MY beliefs is that nothing happens by accident. Our purpose of being on this wonderful planet is to grow and expand our Soul, and everything, literally everything, is an opportunity to do so. We each come here with our own plan for growth, and we will each get opportunities to succeed. If we overlook the opportunities, the Universe will keep sending us chances, many times increasing the pain until we finally wake up.

Life does not spare anyone, and I sincerely mean anyone. Even people who grow up with amazing childhoods and adulthoods can face a curveball when they least expect it. Without the skill to handle crisis and trauma, they are relatively defenseless against whatever they are up against, often dismayed that their perfect life is much less than they thought.

We can see someone else's life as better and ours as less fair, but in reality, we all choose our path, guided by the lessons it would teach us. We need to be proud of what we accomplish, not become resentful because someone else's lessons seem less challenging. I have always had this thought that by the end of each of our lives, we all have an equal amount of pain and, thus, growth opportunities.

Another blessing of mine is the lack of envy for other people's lives, and this is just a product of the many extra past lives I have had. Dr. Hawkins believes we come into this incarnation at a certain consciousness level and rarely deviate more than five points in either direction, which is actually profound considering each level is to the tenth power.

We all start each present life going through the various stages of consciousness, and for those of us who have landed here at a higher starting point, we will go through the lower stages much faster with less psychological damage.

For example, I mentioned the relationship where we both had pasts that were similar, stemming from dysfunctional childhoods, and we were both former star athletes and college stars. We both left successful careers in financial services willingly and ended up settling on life coaching. What I gleaned from my experiences was astronomical compared to what he gleaned, and this puzzled me. After all, how could one person learn so much and another so little under the same experiences?

I asked my Spirit Guides one day and was told, "Each of our sponges is a different size depending on the number of past lives. When one sponge is bigger and can soak up so much more, the other sponge is much smaller, so the amount soaked up will be much smaller."

This not only made perfect logical sense, but it also made me aware of how critical it is not to try to make someone see what appears obvious to someone else. We are all on our own journey, on our own path, at our own level of consciousness.

One is not better than the other; it simply is just where the person is, and we should all reserve judgment.

* * *

> *Not only is it a lesson in futility to try to change or fix someone, but it is not our right to try to do so.*

The idea of each of us having our own sponge size really resonated with me. I have spent my entire life coaching, mentoring, parenting, teaching, and doing everything possible in my romantic relationships to get my partner to see what I saw. In truth, it was my ego believing I had the power to make someone see and the right to do so. It was never my right or my job.

My therapist once said to me, "Tricia, you need to stop falling in love with someone's potential and fall in love with who they are right in front of you." This was a theme I played over and over.

As a person who saw love as parental, I always saw the best in my partners and believed in them, often more than they believed in themselves. I also believed in the persona they created and fell in love with that persona, even though their actual self didn't even resemble who they said they were.

When we fall in love with potential instead of reality, we are both setting ourselves up for disappointment and setting the other up to feel less than they are. We all present our best selves to new potential partners; some of us present a persona that closely matches our true selves, putting our best sides forward, while others present a fictitious person who doesn't come close to who they actually are, often unaware that the persona is not the "real deal."

Given time, the "real" person will emerge. The challenge for those of us who trust so readily is to wait long enough to see the authentic person before falling in love. In almost all cases, within three to six months, with enough contact, the real person will emerge, especially if you pay close attention to how they handle conflict and stress.

Historically, I have trusted others unconditionally and not trusted myself when I should have. In all cases, both platonic and romantic relationships, there were huge red flags that I should have questioned. I either chose to overlook them in my need to find love or didn't even recognize them until I was already in love.

Most of my relationships have a very similar trajectory: I meet a man; he tells me who he is. The words veer heavily from the actions. If I see it, I overlook my instinct; if I question it, the answer, though mostly vague and shallow, satisfies me. I get emotionally attached and invested. Then, between months three and six, an egregious act occurs that hurts me to the core. Instead of facing reality and breaking up at that point because I know I deserve better, I hang in there and spend the rest of the relationship parenting the other person toward maturity and becoming who they claimed to be.

Obviously, this never works, and even when they profess commitment towards growth, the genuine commitment is towards managing me and maintaining things as they are. In the end, nothing ever changed, no one ever grew. The person never resembled who they claimed to be and, as Maya Angelou said, "If someone shows you who they are, believe them the first time." Anyone can invent a story; living it is the key. Actions always speak louder than words ... always.

I have allowed myself to be burned so many times, from friends to family to romantic relationships, that one would think I wouldn't trust anyone. The reality is I have historically trusted blindly—everyone except me. Obviously, I have it backward, another dysfunctional childhood remnant.

When you grow up in a dysfunctional family system, the fallout is often that you can't trust yourself. After all, if Stepfather could molest me, and I somehow saw him as the victim, trusting myself would be impossible since my programming conditioned me to tell myself untruths. Likewise, I gave Mother a million chances, being an obedient daughter, financially and emotionally, until she literally took her last breath, willing myself to forgive her because "she did her best."

The advantage of this attitude is that I have never had regrets. The disadvantage is that I was lying to myself. A more honest approach would have been that, despite the treatment I received in childhood, it was wrong to experience jealousy and to be undermined by one's mother; that Mother was an emotional wrecking ball my entire life; however, I stood by her because I wanted no regret. I had similar dialogues with myself, though my story has changed a lot since my husband's death and my healing.

Chapter 7

*Once our Soul is slowly revealed, we change
into our authentic self, and the story we told
ourselves about our past changes as well, replaced
by a new story that speaks the Truth.*

✸

FOR MOST OF my life, Mother was the avenger, the evil Mother who wreaked havoc on all of us, the witch full of hatred and darkness, sending out her low energy vibrations to anyone within range. Much of the story is still true. My reaction and understanding are now different. Yes, Mother was bitter, angry, and often embraced victimhood, as well as being jealous, unloving, and invalidating. However, she was also bright, funny, conscientious when sober, neat, and organized. Within her limited scope, she did love us.

Mother herself suffered, having grown up with a mother who was tough and abrasive but enabling, and a father who doted on her. She fell off her pedestal when she became pregnant at 16, ostracized by the Catholic school she attended, suffering the embarrassment amongst her peers and her own mother, who felt disgraced.

Not having the tools to weather her emotional storm, she lashed out, got pregnant again within eleven months, and literally sealed her fate by the age of 17. My biological father, still a child himself, was not content to play father for very long, and after an ultimatum to stay at home and help or leave and never see his kids again, he chose the latter. This sounds valiant of Mother, but I'm sure it was more about her needs than my brother and me.

So, my father stayed away as he was told. I never even knew of my biological father (safely kept in my mother's vault) until the year of my older son's birth, when I received a letter in the mail from my grandmother with a newspaper clipping of a murder suicide. I did not know who the people were, and when I called my grandmother to ask and to hear, "That is your real father," I felt shock and more shame. As you can expect, I gasped because of the brutality of the murder suicide, but I was told not to worry because "He was dying of cancer, and they planned it," as if this was a normal exit point!

The conversation ended with that, stuffed into the vault. I do not know if Mother knew. The clipping came from Grandmother, so I never told her, and in fact, never even told Chuck or anyone; I just put it safely in my vault and went on.

Several years ago, I was at a reading with Rosalie, lamenting yet another failed, toxic relationship, and my biological father came through, apologizing for "my abandonment issues." Up to this point, I didn't even realize I had abandonment issues. Months later, I discovered I did, despite being so self-sufficient and independent.

At the same reading, I was shown how his life played out. He sent money and birthday cards to Mother for us that we never received. After we moved and he couldn't find us, he sent money to my grandmother for us, which she kept and never mentioned. He even described watching my brother's football games, perfectly describing the field layout and where he stood to watch. My brother later confirmed that he remembers being approached by a stranger at one of his games who shook his hand as if he knew him. He knew all about my running and was very remorseful for not stepping in.

After he remarried, his new wife was against it, and he claimed to have carried this regret in his heart his entire life. They also gave a snapshot of what his life was like with our half-siblings, and it turns out he was a raging, physically abusive alcoholic as well; it appears the alcohol gene is prevalent in my brother and me, though none of my siblings or I have ever chosen to escape through addiction, thankfully.

Initially, hearing I had abandonment issues, I wasn't on board, deciding the reading did not add up. How could someone like me, who was so resilient and never acted needy and never asked for anything, suffer from the inability to be alone? It made little sense until it did. From this, I learned we can't rush growth, and hearing the words is useless until we can integrate them.

Finally, I was ready, and it was a huge wake-up call. I was at the last stages of toxic relationship number two, and each time I was resolute that I was done, he would come back, and I would agree. I knew he was not the best for me, but I loved him, and I didn't understand why I allowed him back in when he lied, had addiction issues, and possibly even stole from me.

In the end, being with someone who treated me so poorly was better than being alone. When we finally ended things because he was playing his push-and-pull emotionally unavailable game like a pro, I decided I had had enough and actually deserved better.

✹ ✹ ✹

Until we truly believe we are worthy, we will continue to choose the same type of psychological partner over and over.

We all deserve better, and it's important not only to know one's needs but also to have the willingness to walk away if the person is incapable or unwilling to meet them. This doesn't mean our relationship partner has responsibility for completing us, making us whole—this is entirely our own job. What it means is we need to enter a relationship when we are completely whole, or at least when our willingness is there. If we are completely whole, we will no longer be vibrating with those who aren't, and so who we attract will be someone of equal wholeness and a willingness to grow.

If we find ourselves in a relationship, we can practice discernment and see the red flags as they are appearing instead of months later when things fall apart. We will have the inner strength to ask the tough questions and be more willing to guard our hearts until it is safe to let someone in.

When we achieve this level of completeness, we can recognize our mature relationship needs and the power to set boundaries and leave if necessary. Conversely, if we are coming from a place of lack and have emotional holes, we will hang on for dear life and unconsciously overlook glaring flaws and red flags, preferring the toxic relationship over being alone, even if we are unhappy more often than not.

Accepting people for who they are and not trying to make them into someone we need is the cornerstone of healthy relationships. We can't do this if we invest in staying attached at all costs.

✺ ✺ ✺

We must learn to forgive. He who doesn't learn to forgive deprives himself of the beauty to Love.

A cornerstone of acceptance is accepting oneself; accepting oneself is forgiving oneself, which takes so much more than just saying the word. Much of my shame resulted from my family dynamic. Some of it, though, resulted from the survival choices I made along the way, particularly until my mid-twenties, choices that have caused me incredible shame. Nothing horrible, but it was definitely not in line with my Higher Self, and I needed to forgive myself to forgive others.

What I learned about the relationship I just spoke about was that, besides knowing I need to trust myself foremost and have stronger boundaries, I also needed to forgive myself for all the perceived sins from my childhood. By forgiving this man each time he did something that violated my values, I was, in effect, allowing myself to forgive myself. I realized his behavior was unconscious and the leftover effects of life experiences with a smaller sponge. Where I once took things he did personally, I realized it was never that; it was just him being himself.

Does this mean I should allow someone like that back into my life? Absolutely not. We are vibrating at very different frequencies, and as such, my goal of an equal relationship with this person is impossible at this point.

Is he a horrible person for what he did? No, he's just still living out his childhood trauma the best way he knows how. From this, not only was I able to forgive myself, but I could also authentically forgive my parents, family, friends, and anyone else who has ever hurt me, manipulated me, or taken advantage of me; after all, I played my role perfectly in each drama, and they were just playing their role as well.

What I find so interesting is that all my life, I felt forgiveness for others; however, it was coming from a place of ego, not my Higher Self. Once I could connect the fact that my ego was doing the forgiving—and I knew this because of the guilt it helped assuage—then I could change my lens.

Now, my forgiveness is heart-based and authentic, coming from my Higher Self rather than my ego. This has allowed me to see Mother through my heart and not my head, and it has fostered a completely different lens. This new lens allows me to see Mother from her point of view, which has afforded me more compassion, empathy, and understanding for where she was throughout my childhood.

It doesn't take away all that has happened, but it allows me to see things differently and more accurately. This year was the first time in my life that I actually missed Mother, all because my lens had shifted.

Chapter 8

Judging a person does not define who they are. It defines who you are.

—Wayne Dyer

❋

JUDGMENT AND FORGIVENESS go hand in hand, and it's hard to stop judgment if you can't authentically forgive. Some say that every time you judge someone else, you are, in fact, on some level judging yourself, usually your shadow that you have disowned. We all have a shadow that we try everything in our power to avoid seeing.

When we disown some of our parts we don't wish to acknowledge, we will see these traits in another person and perceive them negatively. The sooner you make peace and friends with your disowned parts, the sooner you can become whole and truly authentic.

Every human on the planet is a mix of dark and light, and making believe we are all light under every circumstance is silly. This knowledge has given me a much deeper sense of understanding and compassion towards youthful offenders.

Who knows how I might have behaved under the same circumstances?

People have to suffer the consequences of their choices and actions, but as a society, it doesn't mean we can't have a level of understanding and compassion, recognizing that on any day, we all have the same potential if given the same stimulus.

Finding the power to forgive myself has been extremely liberating and has helped move me away from codependency, which was ego-driven, and towards my authentic Self. I can now say no freely. I don't feel the urge to fix, and, most importantly, I finally understand the concept that one must love oneself before one can truly love another.

Part of loving oneself is to stop judging oneself and everyone else on the planet. Very early on, I knew this, but I wasn't nearly as concise in the execution as I could have been. I remember one day when my older son was three or four years old, looking outside my window and seeing the neighbors doing something with their kids that I would never allow.

I remember being more of an observer and not an active participant in the scene, and asking myself, "Why do people care how other people parent?" It came to me immediately when I realized we care because, on some level, if we parent differently than someone else, since the ego claims that only one person could be right, we immediately make the other wrong, or we would have to be wrong. Our ego never wants to be wrong or accept that often there is more than one right.

✳ ✳ ✳

One of the freeing moments in life is when we find the courage to let go of the things we can't change.

Letting go is another fundamental quality of a person who is living with Inner Peace. For me, letting go of people has always been a challenge; I often took the failure of a connection as a personal failure on my part, rather than a simple fact of life. I was always adjusting to the other person to make things work, fearing I would lose them.

In truth, most of these relationships were an excellent example of the premise that we allow people into our lives who treat us exactly as we treat ourselves. If we subconsciously are coming from a place of shame or lack, the people we attract will only exacerbate these feelings and become a mirror of shame and lack.

This manifests most often in romantic relationships. Even in friendships, I would ask for nothing, subconsciously afraid of rocking the boat and alienating the person. This often resulted in me attracting the very people who took advantage of me. Sometimes, the manipulation was conscious, but in many other situations, the person was again just being themselves, seeking to have their needs met in any way possible.

Can I blame them for reaching out and my reaching back? It's very easy to do this but very misguided. In any relationship, both parties play their role, or there wouldn't be a relationship at all, since by definition, a relationship requires relating. If you have ever been with someone when things started off with a positive connection and later felt "off," what probably occurred is that you were no longer relating, which really means you were no longer vibrating on the same frequency.

✺ ✺ ✺

Programmed patterns largely dictate human behavior and will repeat until we become conscious of these patterns.

"Compulsion to Repeat," as stated by Freud, says that until we uncover our unconscious motivations and heal our core wounds, we are likely to repeat them over and over. I can certainly attest to this from a very personal perspective. I have an external deep dislike for entitlement, self-centeredness, victimhood, and denial, and I overtly recoil from people who carry these traits.

Despite my profoundly negative feelings, every romantic relationship and many platonic relationships have attracted just these people. Why on earth would I let this happen when it has caused me nothing but stress, hurt, and frustration my entire life? The answer is simple: each person was an opportunity to uncover my own disowned traits, and by doing so, I healed and transformed.

We all have these emotional triggers, and while my weakness is alcoholics and the myriad of emotions that go along, others attract betrayal by cheating, or perhaps physical abuse. While I would never allow a cheater or a physical abuser to stay, you might never allow an alcoholic to stay. We each have our zero tolerance for specific things, and those we allow are the areas we need to focus on.

In reality, while I disliked all the traits of alcoholism, my shadow was longing for the ability to be less responsible, to allow myself to fall back on someone else, and to be less mature, not unlike the very qualities in alcoholics that I detested. Once I saw the reality of my shadow, I could then move towards the falsehoods I believed about myself: I was more resilient than most, I am responsible for everyone, I have no one to fall back on, and I am all alone.

Identifying what's in our suitcase and going through it piece by piece is hard work but spectacularly healing and necessary. I contend that without addressing the root of our limiting beliefs, we will continue to play out the same scene throughout our lives, never fully understanding why things happen as they do.

The "little girl" in me longed to change the outcome of emotional neglect at the hands of alcoholics in childhood. The reality is that we can't fix the past with the present; we can only heal the past and not repeat it.

Chapter 9

Everything is energy, right down to the smallest blade of grass. As energy, we vibrate. What determines our vibration is our thoughts and feelings.

❋

WE ARE ALL energy; everything in the Universe is energy. I know that to many, this might seem impossible; however, quantum physics has proven this to be true. Everything is vibrating, even the chair you're sitting on or a rock in the park. Our human eyes cannot perceive this, yet with a strong enough microscope, you would see the atoms that make up the chair or rock vibrating and moving around. Just because we can't see it does not make it untrue.

Albert Einstein famously said, "Everything is energy, and that's all there is to it. Match the frequency of the reality you want, and you cannot help but get that reality. It can be no other way. This is not philosophy. This is physics." We are all entangled, so every vibration influences every other vibration in the Universe.

Some say that, at the core of all, pain and suffering is the energy and vibration of fear, while the core of all joy and inner peace is the energy and vibration of Love. Fear and Love are opposite ends of the vibrational scale. When I say fear, I don't mean the external feeling of fear when you are in danger, which is justified; I mean the internal state of being fearful, coming from a place of lack and a feeling of disconnection from your Higher Self, Higher Power, and everything and everyone else. When I say Love, I am not referring to the external feeling or action of loving someone, though this is important. Instead, I mean the internal state of being Love. Being Love manifests itself in a sense of connectedness to our Higher Self, Higher Power, everything, and everyone. The lens through which we see the world—fear or Love—will create the reality in which we live.

When living from a state of fear, we are living in our ego; when living from a state of Love, we are living in our Higher Self. If we grow up in families that were emotionally abusive and emotionally neglectful, we may not be living our truth or our Higher Self. In fact, for many of us, we buried our Higher Self to stay safe. When this happens, our ego steps in and creates emotional blockades or "wet blankets," as I call them—a kind of fortress around our authentic self—so we can live in an environment that might otherwise emotionally destroy us.

These defenses served many of us well in childhood, and even as adults, they might have propelled us toward success from society's perspective. Ego defenses for others might have done the opposite, making you believe that trying was futile because, after all, nothing changes. Both outcomes are significantly damaging to our long-term Inner Peace and to living one's life authentically. What saved us in childhood often causes the most damage in adulthood, and mainly in the two arenas that matter the most: relationships and career.

Thoughts, emotions, and actions all have their own vibrational frequencies. If you live in the world of negative thought, you will vibrate at that negative level. Most of us have felt the presence of someone who makes us feel uncomfortable. Many times, we cannot put our finger on "why," but we just know something doesn't seem safe. The person's energy affects our energy, and we feel anxious or unsettled.

This is our Higher Self or intuition alerting us to the energy of this person, letting us know this person is vibrating at an energetic frequency that feels off. Most of us have also been in the presence of someone we've just met and feel so comfortable and at ease. Despite just meeting them, we feel safe and often want to get closer. This person is vibrating at a high frequency. The attraction is positive and has a calming effect.

Any fear-based energy will always feel dense; a Love-based energy will always feel light. We all can read energy once we know it's "real," and I find it very beneficial to help guide decisions about people and other areas of my life.

If you have ever gotten an inner feeling that something feels off or, perhaps out of the blue, you have a thought, you should not go somewhere with a person or stop an activity you were considering—heed your own internal warning. This, too, is energy or intuition, and it's a barometer we all have inside us if we choose to listen.

In this circumstance, belief is important because, by not doing something, we might not always know what we avoided, but we need to trust it was in our highest and best interest not to do it, even without evidence. This is often the power of meditation. By calming our minds, thoughts, and feelings, we are opening up the pathway to our Higher Self and higher frequency.

The most important thing to remember is that our ego never has our best interests in mind from a Soul perspective. The ego operates from a place of lack and fear, and as a result, every thought, feeling, and action will be negatively impacted.

If you want to change your lens, you must change the energy within. Our Higher Self is always waiting to be set free from the ego and the heaviness of the "wet blankets" that cover our true, authentic self. These blankets are burdensome and uncomfortable, weighing us down just like how negative emotions make us feel heavy. An important thing to remember is that it is our birthright to be free and light and to live our authentic self; that is why we came to this planet.

We all have the power within us to overcome anything that has happened to us in the past. When we came into this world, we were only Light and Love. Our programming messed it up; we are not messed up.

❉ ❉ ❉

Attachment is the source of all suffering.

—Buddha

Attachment is an interesting word, in that for most of us, we have been taught to attach to things. How else would we achieve Love, raise children, or stay committed to a cause? While this is true on one level, attachment in Buddha's quote is not a feeling that binds one to a person, thing, cause, ideal, or something similar. It is actually the state of being attached to an outcome.

Why is this so bad? Because the minute we attach to an outcome, we have given away our Inner Peace and Power. That is not to say that a person, thing, or ideal is not important. It is to say that when we identify with these things, we have moved into our ego, which can only come from a place of fear. Attachment is the clinging, the grasping, the emotional demand that something or someone stay as it is so we can feel safe, worthy, or whole.

If we are coming from a place of fear, we are handing over our power and looking outside ourselves to be whole. Nothing outside of ourselves has the power to complete us. The only completeness is the realization that we are already whole, and it's the ego that has made us feel otherwise. When we seek wholeness from a person, place, thing, or attachment, we are setting ourselves up for a lot of pain, and we are telling ourselves subconsciously that "I am not enough."

The minute that tape plays, the reality you will see will represent the fact that you believe on a deep level that you are not enough. This creates a sense of helplessness and unworthiness, and every relationship and decision will reflect this. Thoughts and emotions will determine our internal vibration, where who we are inside will be what we create on the outside.

✳ ✳ ✳

When deep inside you feel unworthy of love, unworthy of abundance, or unworthy of peace, you will live a life of toxic relationships, material lack, and inner turmoil. It can be no other way. Permanent change must come from the inside out; change your programming, change your life.

Everything we do is based on a set of patterns we have learned from childhood programming. If you were told you were "bad" for having negative emotions, you would bury your negative emotions and then often create relationships that have the other person carry the negative emotions you can't own yourself. When you are told that your needs mean nothing, you will often seek partners or even bosses who disregard your feelings and needs. If you could never have boundaries, you would seek people in your world who violate your boundaries. Conversely, if you were told you were worthy, you would pick relationships, bosses, and friends who respect and value you.

When we look back on our lives, we can see the patterns created by our childhood programming. These patterns will continue until we expose and heal them, and new patterns are formed. They correlate with the messages we unconsciously tell ourselves: We're unworthy, we aren't enough, Love comes outside ourselves, we lack connection, our authentic self isn't good enough, I'm bad, I'm damaged, I'm a victim, I'm helpless, etc. The energy of these thoughts and feelings creates the patterns about ourselves, and that energy is what we send out into the world. It's that very energy that creates our reality. It's that energy that attracts toxic partners, narcissistic bosses, ungrateful friends, inner turmoil, chaotic environments, and material lack.

If we reprogram our thoughts by undoing the false messages we were told about ourselves, the world we create will be incredibly different. This is a world where Inner Peace and unconditional Love abound.

Chapter 10

Addiction isn't about people who become addicted to the substance or action; it's about people who become addicted to the act of escaping themselves.

✸

WILLINGNESS IS THE cornerstone of having the courage to face one's demons. Having had alcoholism in my life since early childhood, I have had tremendous exposure to the 12-step program via AA and Al-Anon.

Stepfather quasi hit his bottom, supposedly giving up drinking ten years prior to his death when he was told he would soon die if he didn't. The fear of death sometimes is greater than the fear of living, so he stopped.

Mother never hit her bottom, drank literally until she went into hospice, stopping only because she got access to much better self-medication options with every pain relief known to man. Chuck attended an outpatient program for a few months and was a regular participant in AA programs for years.

I was not completely on board with the 12-step programs until recently since it did little to "save" my husband, and my personal foray into AA as a facilitator was a weekly meeting of people expressing how much life didn't deal them a fair hand—the very thing I had grown up with and needed to get away from. AA seemed like an imperfect solution at best, with no checks or balances to ensure that people were actually working the program effectively. What I have since learned is that without willingness, there isn't any program in the world that will help someone overcome their addictions.

I have changed my views, particularly as I realize that my own spiritual journey was, in fact, my own 12-step program. People aren't successful in the program that begins, not ends, when the substance or action stops, because stopping there overlooks the most important part: spiritual transformation. The program provides a process for spiritual transformation, and if you have the willingness to be honest with yourself, you can be honest with others, and the possibility of success increases dramatically.

I have also learned that success is a very individual thing. What one person can get out of the program might be far different from someone else, but this is a matter of their sponge size more than anything, and it doesn't correlate with a lack of success.

We could all use a 12-step program at some points in our lives, and it is not just about addiction as we know it. This applies to any addiction, even an addiction to the falsehoods of one's ego.

❋ ❋ ❋

It's not the fear of death we fear, but the fear of living. Both are intricately entwined.

Some say that the fear of death is at the core of every other fear. This is another belief I accept. First, the word death for most of us has a negative connotation, conjuring up whatever fears we have about where we go after we die. For some of us, the fear is in the emptiness of nothingness, and for others, it's wondering if our God will judge us "good" or "bad" and either send us to hell or heaven. Seen from a Soul perspective, death is just a human word, made up to express and communicate the passing of someone. If one believes we are a spiritual being with a human body, we can never die and, despite the human word, there is no death.

As John Lennon stated, "In death, we are just switching cars." This is unquestionable to me after thousands of hours with mediums who have documented this. The Soul or Essence never dies; it never leaves per se, it simply transforms to a different dimension, since to form a body, one must have a denser energy or vibration. The Soul is too light to create a body in this other dimension and of little concern when a body is no longer needed.

I have heard countless stories about near-death experiences, and universally, they all involved feeling the Light and energy of complete acceptance, with an indescribable sense of Love and wholeness. There was a pull towards that Light and a sense of familiarity, as if being "home." Most did not readily want to go back to their body because the unconditional Love was so profound. Upon entering their human body and returning to this world, the person's life has universally changed monumentally. The reason: the fear of death is gone, and along with it, the fear of living.

Arguably, if one fears death, one also fears life. Fearing death causes us to live in fear and, as *A Course in Miracles* states, "There are only two ways to live, in fear or in Love." On the surface, this might seem too simplistic and, therefore, not possibly true, but if you ponder it for a minute, it makes sense. If you have any fear, you are moving from Love, and Love is truly the only purpose of being here. It's actually the foundation of most biblical teachings, despite whatever fear-based doctrines might have resulted from its analysis. Another truism is that the ego only knows fear. Knowing this helps us realize where our beliefs, thoughts, and actions are coming from.

Do you wake up each day and believe you have everything you need? That you're never alone? That everything and everyone Divinely connects? That the only thing our God or Higher Power asks of us is to be the best version of our true self?

Or do you wake up and feel alone? Do you wonder what problems you will face today and whether you have the strength to handle them? Are you feeling disconnected in life, both from your inner being and others? Do you even know who your true self is?

The former thoughts are based on Love, the latter on fear. You can see from the fear-based perceptions that, before you even get out of bed and often while dreaming, one's entire life is vibrating at a level of lack if you are predominantly acting from your ego. You can see how the Law of Attraction plays out here. Even if the very next action is to say your daily words of positive affirmation, the fear is still running the show, which means the ego is in charge.

The ego is formidable. Ego relies on denial to revise history to support its shaky self-esteem. The only antidote to the false messages the ego tells us is radical self-honesty. The ego never wants to give up control by being honest, because doing so might allow you to see the Divine that is within each of us. Once you see this and experience your own Power and Light, you will desperately want to give up the ego for your Truth and the opportunity for Inner Peace.

This is the reason people chase addictions, or at least from Dr. Hawkins's perspective, which believes that addiction only serves to lower the blocks that keep us from our internal Light and being. It's the Light we're actually chasing, versus the drug itself.

On the surface, it might seem far-fetched, but if you think about it, why does the 12-step program work? It works because one of the first steps is surrendering yourself to a Higher Power, whatever that might mean to you. It is saying I know I can't do this alone, essentially attempting to take the ego out of the equation to allow your Light to shine through, a Light we all have, despite what we have been told and the poor decisions and choices we might have made along the way.

One's Higher Self is never less than pure. The ego is not a fan of Truth, and, mostly, anything the ego says or does is based on falsehood. After all, it's coming from a place of fear. As a minor example, let's say you have an unconscious sense of lack, so you project this onto your neighbor and decide you dislike your new neighbor because the neighbor is wealthy and has a lot of material possessions. Your ego might look at him or her and determine that they are materialistic, money-hungry, and therefore not someone you would want to befriend.

The ego is actually feeling threatened, less than, and inferior because the neighbor has more, and so the ego judges to make itself "feel better." In reality, this is just the ego's ploy and most likely entirely false. Conversely, if you are in unison with your Higher Self, you might not even give the new neighbor's material items a second glance, more concerned with who the neighbor is as a person, not judging but getting to know them. The first is born out of fear, based on one's own personal lack; the second is born out of Love, only possible when your emotional cup is already full.

In the end, what we give attention to is what matters to us. If we focus on what we own, where we live, how others perceive us, the car we drive, the house we own, the money we have, the ego is in charge. It's not wrong or bad to want these things; it's only detrimental if we identify with them.

A Course in Miracles states that all special relationships move us away from our Higher Self, whether it is a romantic relationship where we derive our self-worth or any other relationship—religion, money, our car, or a home—where our self-worth is reflected.

As with all things in this world, it's the intention that matters. Striving to have material things to make us comfortable is perfectly fine. The importance is not to let those things define who we are inside. Many people believe that to be a truly spiritual being, we must live with little. This is not the case; what matters is the perception of what these things mean to us. Intention behind one's thoughts and actions is always the key.

Chapter 11

How you love yourself is how you teach others to love you.

—Rupi Kaur

✸

A LACK OF SELF-LOVE is at the root of most human suffering. I have always felt extremely confident, with high self-esteem, and fully capable of climbing any obstacle. The glass ceiling I never considered, and I never felt marginalized because I am a female and never cowered to a man, ever. I was always resilient, and little did I know, I was hiding from myself.

When I realized on some deep core level that my authentic feeling towards myself was feeling "worthless," I was beyond shocked. It couldn't possibly be so, yet it had to be because I said it. This was devastating for me to accept. I had built a fortress of impermeable emotional walls that reinforced my belief system of worth, and it was hard to fathom that it was all false. The problem is you can't unsee what you've seen, so a new journey of discovery began.

First, I had to accept that if this was false, what else might be false? It was at this point that the whole carefully constructed house of cards came tumbling down. I started accepting the truth about myself, which allowed me to accept the truth about everyone else in my life.

Mother was horrible at times, but also loving in her own way. Stepfather worked hard, but he abused me; one will never compensate for the other. I was strong but not resiliently gifted. I was just well-armored and actually incredibly sensitive. My brothers were not less emotionally capable, and I wasn't responsible for them. My friends were taking and not giving, and this was not OK. Romantic relationships were toxic, and labeling them in any way mattered not. They weren't right for me, no matter what the disorder was or wasn't.

Finding a label to blame the other just serves to take the focus off one's own complicity. Nobody is truly a victim of any relationship; we are all culpable and play our own part. After all, we chose involvement with this person, and acknowledging this is the first step towards identifying life patterns.

This is not to ignore clear abuse by any means. Abuse is never acceptable in any way. This simply means that our vibration aligned with theirs, so the only way to heal is to look inward. I was literally transforming before my eyes each day, and it was very hard. The stories I had told myself (and the lies those stories created) no longer resonated.

Many friends dropped away, and I tried my best to let them go, not hanging onto an attachment that wasn't serving my highest and best good. This was incredibly stressful for me with my newly acknowledged attachment issues. Yet, I persevered and, as some say, when people drop away, we create space for the right people to fill it.

Sure enough, within months, new friends entered my life in a completely balanced way. I still cared deeply for my family but have released the self-imposed obligation to bail them out for all their financial stresses. Willing to be there emotionally, but nothing more.

I have made peace with my own failings and shortcomings and the human mistakes I have made along the way. Instead of trying to be someone, I am just seeking peace and wholeness, realizing that both are my most treasured possessions and goals.

✢ ✢ ✢

Coincidence is God's way of remaining anonymous.

—Albert Einstein

Some say that "Nothing in life is ever random. Everything that happens is supposed to happen. Trust the process." This is a challenge for most humans who learned from a young age that to be an adult, we must make things happen, we are the captain of our own ship, and for those of us who suffered severe emotional trauma, control was a necessary wingman to stay relatively sane. My internal edict was to control life so that nothing bad could happen.

Eternally optimistic, many perceived me as pessimistic because, from early childhood, I was always searching the environment for landmines and took actions to prevent myself from stepping on any. This behavior carried over into my adult life, and although it allowed me to see the consequences of my actions much further down the road than most, it also kept me in a state of control and fight mode.

High stress was my normal homeostasis, and I did not know I was in this state until I was told that I had high blood pressure despite being an avid runner logging over fifty miles a week, vegetarian, vitamin popper, and spiritual seeker of peace, at 5'6" and 115 pounds. As my physician said one day when I was fighting taking medicine, "There's nothing we can tweak to help normalize your blood pressure; you're already doing all the suggestions we would normally prescribe." I was told I would need to take a blood pressure medication as a reminder to breathe, stay calm, and surrender. Years later, after releasing everything to my Higher Power, I no longer have high blood pressure.

As my transformation strengthened, opportunities started coming my way. I found Dr. Hawkins's teachings while searching for Inner Peace, and found a local study group. I met an amazing person, someone I'm sure I've known over many lifetimes. She and I just get each other spiritually.

From there, I started hearing about *A Course in Miracles* and saw it, too, was being taught locally. This course teaches how to choose Love as the decision-maker in life, versus the ego, which always comes from a place of fear. We are all on a spiritual journey in this Earth School, and while there are many other paths to becoming more spiritually aligned, this one resonates on a very deep level for me. I am now an active ACIM student, traveling two hours to Yellow Springs, where I have the absolute joy of spending an hour and a half with other like-minded students.

During this significant period of transformation, I was also finding myself moving further from the organized religion I had practiced for the previous 20 years. Not that I didn't believe in the doctrines, but it just didn't seem to meet my spiritual needs fully. I still give back in various ways, including as a youth leader and on councils and even on the church governing board, but I was struggling with my spiritual fit.

What I have found is that for me, many places help meet my spiritual needs, and all are necessary for me to meet my needs fully. We don't need to commit to a spiritual avenue; we all need to find what works for us. At the Spiritualist services, there are offers of energy healings on a free will basis, and I would ask each time for Inner Peace. I visited many clergy with this desire, asking each how to fully let go. No one could tell me.

I recognized I had no one to have my back since I was six, and to give up that control seemed impossible. I also knew this was my ego. I wanted to "Let go, Let God," but I just didn't know how to relinquish that small speck of control that inhibited my Peace. At night, I prayed. I meditated for this release while I ran, and I read everything I could to allow myself to give up control. Still, I felt resistant until one evening in November.

I had just gotten home from running, so I was still in shorts. I needed to sterilize something in the grass so my dog, Lilly, would not step in it. After boiling a large pot of water, I grabbed it off the stove with two mitts. I took one step, and most of the pot of boiling water splashed all over my bare leg.

What's amazing is I saw it happen to myself as if I were observing it play out. I watched it happen to my body from afar; I was no longer in my body, instead across the room, but my mind was with me, not with my body. Calmly, I remember the thoughts passing through my head: "Oh, this is going to hurt," and then "I guess I won't be running for a while." Then, I became present and "jumped back into my body."

Water was all over the hardwood floor, and I immediately started drying it, using most of a paper towel roll. I then went and poured the remaining water on the spots outside, immediately burning the grass. When I finally had the guts to look at my leg, I was expecting the worst, and here's the crazy part—my leg had not burned, it never turned red, it never hurt.

It was literally as if it had never happened.

I didn't ask for Divine Intercession, but this surely was one. From that day forward, I knew and now know that anything is possible, that I was not walking alone, and that our bodies are not our reality. I have found Faith and Inner Peace, a Peace we all deserve and can all have if we strive towards this goal.

Where before I felt anxiety in my heart at the prospect of being alone, now I feel a fullness that I can only describe as deep self-love, whether alone or not, a Love I never knew existed. I know I am now in alignment and have nothing to fear. Life will unfold exactly as it unfolds.

I started planning this book about five years ago after writing answers to Quora and realizing I had a lot to say. I thought finding true Love would be my last chapter. It turns out that it was actually self-love.

Every cliché written about love and life comes back to "you must love yourself first before you can love anyone else," and this is *almost* 100 percent correct. What is 100 percent correct is that you can only love another from the level of self-love you have.

If you engage in self-hate, you will pick a partner or friends who mirror this about yourself. Conversely, if you know your worth and value, you will pick people to mirror those qualities. From this, it is easy to see how we make our relationship choices.

I have finally found self-love—the love that doesn't break up with you, manipulate, lie, steal, abuse—is the love that stands the test of time and will always be here. It is the inner Light that connects us all.

Despite all that has happened to me, I still believe in Love at all levels. The difference now is I will not sell myself short and settle for less than what I give. I will use discernment and make sure words and actions match up. I will only bring one casserole to the potluck instead of four, and know it's enough. I will set my boundaries and love myself enough to leave when someone disrespects my values and boundaries. I now see the world through the lens of Love, not fear.

My hope is you can choose this, too.

Acknowledgments

I AM DEEPLY grateful to the many wonderful individuals whose love, wisdom, and support have guided me throughout my spiritual journey and the writing of this book.

I would like to express my deepest gratitude to Igniting Souls for providing the most meaningful platform to bring my book to life. Your expertise throughout the publishing journey has been invaluable. Thank you for believing in my vision and helping make it a reality.

To my husband, Chuck, with sincere gratitude and love for giving me the very best curriculum for learning in the school of life. Our life together has afforded me the opportunity for the greatest growth and has provided my most valuable lessons, for which I thank you.

A special thank you to Rosalie Strawcutter, a gifted clairvoyant medium, whose insights have helped me understand my life in profound and meaningful ways. You mean the world to me, and I am proud to call you a friend. To my spiritual sister, Mary Greene, your unwavering presence and love have been an anchor through it all. Joe Cimoch, your wisdom in leading ACIM has illuminated my path and provided clarity at every turn.

I want to express my deepest gratitude to my friend, Jeff DeRoberts. Through all the ups and downs of life, Jeff has been by my side, offering support, laughter, and friendship when I needed it most. Our bond is unshakeable, and it's impossible to imagine this journey without him.

I would like to thank Bob Peters for graciously allowing us to meet each week at Phoenix Books Clintonville, a space that nurtures growth and community. Nancy Kirchofer, your beautiful facilitation of Dr. Hawkins's teachings has helped me see the world with new eyes.

To my dear book group friends—Madonna, David, Marilyn, Bob, Rahkee, Chetan, Rich, Trish, Andrew, Joseph, Maggie, Katherine, Rev. Clarence, Rebecca, Jim, and Doug— thank you for being such a loving and supportive witness to my spiritual journey and for helping me along this path.

I am incredibly grateful to Gail Lichtenfels for opening Epic Books each Thursday night for our Yellow Springs ACIM group, providing a space for learning and connection.

To my many dear friends, especially Krista, Samantha, Brenda, Beth, Scott, Steve, Deb, Rita, and Anne, your love and friendship have been a constant source of strength and encouragement.

Thank you to Rebecca Manns, Angel Reader, for your spiritual guidance and unwavering support. Mystic Laura Scott, your energy healings and support in helping me discover my life plan have been transformative and truly invaluable. I would like to extend my heartfelt thanks to Psychic Medium Bee Herz for your insightful guidance. Your wisdom has been instrumental in helping me navigate a path toward a more beneficial and fulfilling future.

I would like to express my deepest gratitude to the First Community Church Youth Program and Camp Akita for the unwavering support you have provided to my children and for the profound impact you've had on our lives. Your guidance, care, and unconditional love have not only shaped their growth but have also supported me in ways that words can hardly express.

To my brothers, David, Kenny, and Bruce, and their spouses, Paul (David) and Debi (Bruce), your light in my life has been a constant source of joy and grounding. To Patty, Jeff, Steven, Marcia, Amelia, Kayla, and Colton, thank you for understanding the true value of family and for always being there with love and support.

A heartfelt thank you to Tim, Sharon, Sarah (Alex), Rachel (Alex), Tom, Jane, Chris, and Judy for your continued efforts to maintain a strong relationship with my boys, which has been a great support to me.

To each of you, I offer my heartfelt gratitude. Your presence has helped shape my journey, and I could not have done this without you.

With love and appreciation,

Tricia

About the Author

TRICIA BAXLEY IS a passionate advocate for personal growth and healing with over 25 years of experience in the financial services industry and transformation life coaching. A devoted mother of two amazing boys, Tricia holds degrees in finance and psychology, which have shaped her unique approach to understanding human behavior. In her book, she shares her personal journey from trauma to triumph, exploring the stories we tell ourselves and uncovering the limiting beliefs that hold us back.

Tricia is a Certified MBTI Practitioner and a Certified Life Coach, empowering others to overcome obstacles and embrace their full potential. She is a proud member of the International Coaching Alliance, dedicating her life to helping others heal and achieve lasting transformation. Tricia's commitment to serving others is deeply rooted in her belief in the power of personal development and the impact of self-awareness on all aspects of life. Through her work, she continues to inspire those around her to break free from their limitations and create a life of purpose and fulfillment. In addition to her professional pursuits, Tricia is passionate about mission work, intentional travel, and running, which fuels her drive to connect with others and explore the world with purpose.

DISCOVER PERSONALIZED COACHING SESSIONS

Work one-on-one with Tricia in a sacred, compassionate space where deep inner patterns can rise to the surface and be gently rewritten. This is not about fixing — it's about remembering who you were before the world told you otherwise.

Apath4Healing.com

BRING TRICIA TO YOUR NEXT EVENT

Tricia Baxley speaks from a place of lived experience, emotional depth, and spiritual insight. Her talks invite listeners to gently uncover their unconscious beliefs, embrace their authentic selves, and remember their innate wholeness.

To book Tricia to speak, visit:

Apath4Healing.com

GROUP WORKSHOPS/ RETREATS

Experience heart-centered, collaborative workshops designed to awaken truth, foster healing, and invite soul-level transformation through shared stories, guided inquiry, and sacred connection.

Apath4Healing.com

YOU CAN CREATE LASTING CHANGE!

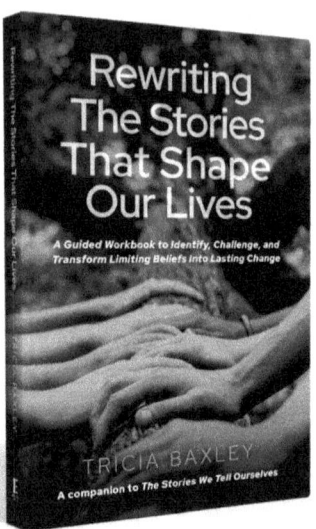

Tricia gently guides you through a step-by-step process of unlearning the stories that kept you small, healing the imprints of early wounding, and returning home to the truth of who you've always been — whole, worthy, and deeply enough.

THIS BOOK IS PROTECTED INTELLECTUAL PROPERTY

The author of this book values Intellectual Property. The book you just read is protected by Instant IP[IP], a proprietary process, which integrates blockchain technology giving Intellectual Property "Global Protection." By creating a "Time-Stamped" smart contract that can never be tampered with or changed, we establish "First Use" that tracks back to the author.

Instant IP [IP] functions much like a Pre-Patent since it provides an immutable "First Use" of the Intellectual Property. This is achieved through our proprietary process of leveraging blockchain technology and smart contracts. As a result, proving "First Use" is simple through a global and verifiable smart contract. By protecting intellectual property with blockchain technology and smart contracts, we establish a "First to File" event.

Protected by Instant IP [IP]

LEARN MORE AT INSTANTIP.TODAY

www.ingramcontent.com/pod-product-compliance
Lightning Source LLC
Chambersburg PA
CBHW052134070526
44585CB00017B/1817